D1222425

CAPITAL MURDER

AN INVESTIGATIVE REPORTER'S HUNT FOR ANSWERS IN A COLLAPSING CITY

CHRIS PAPST

Mechanicsburg, Pennsylvania USA

Published by Sunbury Press, Inc.
50 West Main Street
Mechanicsburg, Pennsylvania 17055

www.sunburypress.com

For information about special discounts for bulk purchases, please contact Sunbury Press Orders Dept. at (855) 338-8359 or orders@sunburypress.com.

To request one of our authors for speaking engagements or book signings, please contact Sunbury Press Publicity Dept. at publicity@sunburypress.com.

ISBN: 978-1-62006-591-4 (Hardcover)
ISBN: 978-1-62006-592-1 (Mobipocket)

Library of Congress Control Number: 2015937881

FIRST SUNBURY PRESS EDITION: May 2015

Designed in the United States of America
0 1 1 2 3 5 8 13 21 34 55

Set in Bookman Old Style
Designed by Crystal Devine
Cover by Lawrence Knorr & Amber Rendon
Cover photo by Mai Kaare
Edited by Amanda Shrawder

Continue the Enlightenment!

CONTENTS

ACKNOWLEDGMENTS

THIS PROJECT WOULD NOT have been possible without the support of my wife, family and good friends. Had I met Paul Beers before his passing, I would have thanked him for his book *City Contented, City Discontented,* which was vital to my understanding of historic Harrisburg. Also, to the man who first suggested I take on this task, and to all those who answered my many questions about this city's more recent past, thank you.

PROLOGUE

AS I GAZED OUT THE WINDOW at 15,000 feet, I wasn't sure what to expect. Minutes later, as I stood in the airport lobby admiring a stunning panorama of the city, my uncertainty turned to skepticism. What I had read online depicted a wonderful place, which contradicted everything I remembered. For me, this was an opportunity to return home after being away for many years. For CBS 21, it was an opportunity to buttress its reporting staff with a local guy.

"Welcome to Harrisburg!" My future news director suddenly appeared. I quickly dropped my thoughts and entered "interview mode."

"Thank you," I replied with a genuine smile. "It's nice to be here."

After shaking hands and exchanging a few more pleasantries, we sought lunch in the city.

My childhood vision of Pennsylvania's capital was of crime, blight and poverty. In the 80s and 90s, it was a place you avoided. But as we exited the highway and entered downtown, it was obvious good things were happening. It was the summer of 2010 and the streets were bustling and clean; the new high-rises perfectly complemented the old architecture and gorgeous riverfront.

1

My news director couldn't understand my shock at city streets lined with small businesses and trendy shops. It was clear; this was not the Harrisburg of my youth.

During lunch, my future boss explained how the city was starting to experience some financial difficulty. He wasn't sure the extent, but he needed an experienced reporter to cover it—just in case. Looking back, I'm so glad I accepted his offer.

Over the following 36 months, what the city endured could only be described as unprecedented in scope, intensity and importance. And what I learned about this remarkable city told an equally remarkable story. Harrisburg's biography began hundreds of years ago, yet it's all connected to the present with brilliance only time possesses.

Most don't realize the vital role Harrisburg played in our nation's early western expansion and the Industrial Revolution, or how those same advantages helped secure the North's victory during the Civil War. General Robert E. Lee understood the value of Harrisburg, which is why he tried to capture it—twice.

The city's postwar momentum helped cast a modern America—turning this small town into an American player. As money poured in from the massive factories and Capitol aristocrats, an ambitious beautification movement merited its one-time moniker "Miniature Paris." But the romance faded as the city's advantages became disadvantages. An inevitable fate plunged the capital into a deep depression. Then at its worst, Mother Nature finished it off in 1972. Soon after, Harrisburg was forgotten and vanished from the American conversation.

Harrisburg's first collapse was not unlike many others in the "rust belt." Foreign competition and domestic demands forced the steel factories and mills to downsize. As residents left the city in search of work, property values fell. The initial decline was gradual, as most residents held out hope. But when the factories and mills closed, most everyone who could leave—did. Poverty replaced prosperity. Plywood replaced glass. Buildings of all zoning types emptied. Idle hands replaced those that were once calloused or manicured.

The depressed housing market encouraged landlords, who had little interest in the city, to buy properties and rent them to whomever agreed to the rate. Unfamiliar demographics emerged, and with it a new criminal element. Harrisburg's schools went from winning national titles and producing Ivy League graduates to graduating few and nearly closing. Race riots ensued. Revenues dried up. The city was forced to drastically raise taxes, ensuring middle and upper-class families would remain in the suburbs.

The vibrant cultural scene vanished. Once proud buildings of varying architectural ages began a new period of perpetual rot. The ornate opera houses and elegant hotels that once hosted American royalty from George Washington to Babe Ruth were razed. Pennsylvania's jewel became America's most indebted city. By the 70s, Harrisburg's middle class population was mostly gone. The city was essentially lifeless. Resurrection seemed such an impossible task no one cared to attempt it.

But the election of 1981 ushered in a young, ambitious, homegrown mayor who sparked an evaporated hope. Mayor Stephen Reed soon embarked the city on a modern renaissance. A god-like persona quickly encircled his administration as national organizations praised his astonishing achievements. The city had roared back to reclaim a portion of its political, economic and cultural relevance. Forbes.com, in 2010, named the Harrisburg area the second best place in America to "Raise a Family." But behind all the accolades and ribbon cuttings, Harrisburg was being gutted.

With few paying attention, bond agencies reaped millions in transfer fees by loaning the city money it could never pay back. Mayor Reed employed creative accounting tricks to shift revenue and hide debt. He faced numerous judges for abusing his mayoral power, but his stranglehold on the political scene shielded him from consequence. While Harrisburg appeared to thrive with new development and start-up businesses, it was incurring a reprehensible debt that no one could—or wanted—to see. At times, the Mayor ran for re-election unopposed. As a result of his "remarkable" achievements, he was once named one of the world's greatest leaders. The political machine he created over 28 years in office was untouchable, and everyone knew it—including him. He became a despot, and the people of this city happily allowed it.

But eventually those accounting tricks could no longer be disguised. Hundreds of millions in debt abruptly came due, and when the treasury was opened, it barely had enough funds to buy a stamp. Harrisburg's prosperity was fake and it suddenly became very real. Months after Mayor Reed left office, a monumental financial collapse—the likes of which America had never seen—had begun. And the most terrifying aspect was that it didn't seem purposeful. City leaders ostensibly wanted Harrisburg to prosper. Their intentions appeared genuine. But like many government actions, intentions are valued more than results—the consequences of sly rhetoric.

And those consequences were severe (except for those responsible). Police and fire departments were slashed to historical lows. As unions fought to get paid, the murder rate spiked to eight-times the national average. Sinkholes felled entire city streets. The aging infrastructure spewed sewage into people's homes. Dark streetlights and potholes were left to heal on their own while buildings collapsed onto sleeping families. Trash cluttered the streets. City-owned lots went years between mowing as landowners were aggressively cited for lack of land maintenance. When the city could no longer afford to fund animal shelters, police used strays for target practice. Month by month, it was unclear if students would even have a school to attend. When the city quit paying its bills so it could pay its workers, the lawsuits mounted.

With Harrisburg in financial free fall, the state took over. For the first time in Pennsylvania history, a receiver was appointed by the Governor—essentially stripping elected officials of their power and city residents of their Constitutional right to representation. More lawsuits were filed. The city's elected leaders even began suing each other. At a time when the people needed help most, lawyers and politicians battled over who would control their deteriorating lives.

After 28 years in office, the "Mayor for Life" lost in a brutal primary to a woman who would also make headlines. In 2009, it was believed Mayor Linda Thompson rode the wave of President Obama's black voter drive. Once in office, that wave proved to be more of a tsunami for the city. Notwithstanding her actions as Mayor, she was a boon for the media. She referred to herself in the third person, made national "worst persons" lists and had a special gift for memorable statements. "We're not opening up our flood gates for some scumbag from Perry County, to dump [trash] for free," she once said of Harrisburg's direct neighbors to the north. The "scumbags" revolted.

By the end of her first term, the city was such a joke that characters like Lewis Butts could become viable mayoral contenders. Candidate Butts promised voters that, as mayor, he'd work to become "the next great black NASCAR driver to come out of central Pennsylvania." He also promised to heavily lobby "Brother Obama" for a giant downtown shark aquarium. Yet, it wasn't until he was charged for vandalizing his opponent's campaign signs that his candidacy finally collapsed. "I spray-painted p-u-s-s on Papenfuse to make it, Papenpuss," he told me in an interview.

In two-and-a-half years, I filed more than 200 reports on Harrisburg's financial collapse and the hapless residents it affected. Nearly every day something news-worthy happened—and little of it good.

Early in my career, I learned the best reporters are able to emotionally separate themselves from their subjects—

allowing for a greater focus on storytelling. Once, while working in Wisconsin, I remember interviewing a shattered mother who just lost her only child to a roadside bomb in Afghanistan. She never got to say goodbye. She never got to say, "I love you" one last time. All she had left to hug was his enlistment picture—made blurry from her tears. During the interview, she achingly rocked back and forth clutching the frame to her chest—barely able to speak. And all I could think was, "What great TV!" Trust me; I'm not proud of it—though, amongst such emotive anguish, it kept me sane.

Yet, despite my built-in safeguards, the abhorrent nature of Harrisburg's demise eventually wore on my psyche. After hundreds of depressing reports, day-after-day, I started to break. This was where I worked. This was my home state's capital city. I had friends who lived and raised families here. I wanted Harrisburg to win. But it seemed impossible.

Although frustrating and dispiriting, I could handle the laughable incompetence of Mayor Thompson, the stubborn ignorance of City Council and even the mis-guided hubris of the state. But the suffering of innocent people simply due to politics and power whittled at my armor.

People were made massively wealthy issuing the bond deals that capsized Harrisburg. But every day at 4:00, I watched as the protagonists who allowed it to happen hopped in their foreign sports sedans and fled town. They left behind a broke and broken city, and not *one person* was held accountable. No arrests. No charges. No indictments. No restitution. The city was financially dead, but apparently no one killed it.

For the longest time, I couldn't understand how a city could have been so financially raped. How could the residents allow it to happen? More importantly, how could the media allow it to happen? In a democracy, where everyone has the right to free speech, and the right to assemble and petition, how is this possible? It took me years to truly understand. And once I finally did, I found it necessary to write this book.

I first met LeTarsha Richardson in early January, 2013, as a bitter cold gripped the area. "This has been bad. This is horrible. I've never been through nothing like this before," she told me. LeTarsha was a single mom of seven kids—mostly school-aged. Due to the city's financial inability to address its aging infrastructure, a sinkhole spanning the width of the street opened in front of her row home. A second soon followed—then a third. The entire block lost water, gas and sewer services. As the river began to freeze, so did the water in her toilets. She and her children spent the day bundled around a portable space heater—waiting.

The Red Cross—not the city—offered the family shelter, but she wasn't interested. "I'm not going to no shelter," she snapped. "I'm not taking my kids to a shelter with people I don't know." Her children couldn't even warm up at school—this was how the family celebrated the New Year.

"We got a Mayor [Linda Thompson] and everything, that's not doing nothing to help this neighborhood. Because I feel this was not our fault. We shouldn't have to supply everything [like utilities] for ourselves." Their misery lasted nearly a week.

Meanwhile, those who rendered the city too crippled to help continued to live the good life with the millions they plundered. No one was ever held accountable for what families like LeTarsha's were forced to endure. It was maddening. Police are quick to track down a teenager who takes a few candy bars from the corner store. But no law enforcement agency from the federal government down to the local district attorney cared to cuff the crooks that murdered Harrisburg.

The public even seemed to follow law enforcement's misguided lead. Countless stories like LeTarsha's only seem to prompt attacks on the media—instead of on those actually responsible. We suddenly became the problem for "exploiting" the crisis. People demanded "good" stories, instead of our focus on the "bad." But if news is defined as the absence of normalcy, then every aspect of Harrisburg's collapse must be covered. We should all fear the day when financial calamity is viewed as normal and charity the abnormal.

Nevertheless, despite legions of stories similar to LeTarsha's, it was my report on October 11, 2011 that finally sent Harrisburg's plight national. It was on that quiet Tuesday night that the dynamics would intensify as City Council filed for Chapter 9 protection. Never before had an American state capital filed for bankruptcy. And I was one of the few to witness it. The subsequent fallout amounted to a reporter's dream, complete with scandals, investigations, a National Civil War Museum and... Wild West Artifacts?

Understand that Harrisburg is not alone; it's just further along. A fake life built on reckless borrowing is now the American standard. We've become a society that no longer values hard work and responsibility as a way to overcome adversity. Instead, we look for quick and easy fixes, which mostly involve the manipulation of money. It seems we no longer see the world for how it really is, but rather how we wished it would be. Can we really expect this lifestyle to last?

This is a book with a purpose. If nothing changes, more Harrisburgs will emerge and the consequences will be disastrous. From a run on the municipal bond market to the necessary succession of vital services, this nation's ability to endure will be tested. The main difference between Pennsylvania's capital city and countless other municipalities is that the 'Burg started sooner and fell harder. My hope is that America learns from Harrisburg's story.

There is nothing unique about Harrisburg—nothing different. What happened here can happen anywhere. No city, state or nation is immune. The harsh reality of basic economics and human nature do not discriminate by any standard. A clear formula for avoiding financial collapse and bankruptcy lies in the pages of this book. The question is, will we adapt?

After that initial job interview with my News Director, I flew back to Wisconsin and started calling real estate agents in Pennsylvania. I remember one lady saying, "Harrisburg has become such a fantastic city. It's not like when you were growing up. You and your wife will love it here. We're not sure what to think about the new Mayor. But our last one did wonderful things. We all thank him."

Despite her optimism, we didn't buy in the city.

1: WITNESSING RARE HISTORY

AS MUCH AS IT WAS FRUSTRATING, it wasn't at all surprising. If anything, it was even expected. Yet still, I couldn't stop myself from blurting out, "Son of a bitchen place!"

With my hands dripping with water, I hopelessly shoved them farther into the empty paper towel holder. Nothing. "Damn it!" I jammed down on the handle and whacked the dispenser on the side. I don't think anyone heard me. Even if they did, who would care? The damn thing had probably been empty for weeks.

With my arms away from my sides, I searched around. One stall still had some unused toilet paper on the roll. The remnants of the old lay scattered on the tired tile floor. I pulled at the final few squares and hurried to dry my hands before anyone walked in. It could be months before the roll was replaced—I didn't need any sour looks. Sure, I could have flicked my wrists. But that doesn't make me feel clean.

As I quickly rubbed my hands opposite the mirror, I glanced down at the familiar crack in the glass. Every time I came here, it seemed just a little bigger—how appropriate. I gently set the damp ball on the small mountain rising out of the trash. For some reason, I took pride in balancing it perfectly so it didn't fall and add to the mess on the floor. Satisfied with its stability, I eased my hand away. It stayed—a success. Then, with a contorted body, I used my right foot to open the door and whispered, "I need out of this damn city."

For a mid-October evening, the air had a pleasant chill. At this point in its history, weather could have been Harrisburg's best feature. The few downtown street lights that still worked were beginning to power on. The quick shuffle of government workers fleeing the Capitol complex had long faded. As with most days, the vanishing glow of their brake lights signaled the closure of business. A fitting word now flashed on city meters: expired. With only a mild breeze to fill the streets, all the "regulars" funneled into city hall. As I walked out of the bathroom, I nodded at those I knew.

Harrisburg's City Council Chambers were not uncommon for a small city: dim, quiet and fatally dull. Nestled at the base of the five-story open atrium of city hall, it is quite forgettable. But this particular night would offer something unique. As reporters and residents took their seats to scan that evening's agenda, they had no idea something unprecedented in American history was about to happen. By night's end, the Legislative branch of America's most indebted city would shock the attentive world.

Harrisburg, itself, is similar to many American capitals. Just a few blocks from city hall, high on a hill, looms the grandeur of a marble and gold dome. A stunningly remarkable building nestled within an ever-sprawling concrete complex. What may make this town a little dissimilar is knowing that a thriving black neighborhood was forcibly razed to accommodate this grand expansion. Then, when hundreds of millions were spent to make the grounds look spectacular, more money was spent to hide it. The Romanesque statues at the main entrance originally had their genitals exposed.

The hastily applied blobs of cement used to calm the public's outcry, exemplifies the mentality of those who dwell within.

Parts of city proper, just down the hill, more or less resembled a third world country. The demise of industry and the state's seizing of real estate have decimated anything resembling a tax base. Ironically, the town which predated and willingly ceded land for the Capitol has been relegated to its forgotten, if not abused, stepchild. Harrisburg's increasingly aging and unemployed population consists largely of those lacking the resources to flee to the suburbs. And it's in those suburbs where elected leaders are accused of exhibiting nothing less than disdain for the city in which they work.

Most everyone is familiar with the drill. Street lights and one way signs whisk state employees into their parking spots by 9:00 and out by 5:00. The transients include a heavily protected Governor who resides in a gated mansion and other elected officials who comprise the largest full-time and second highest paid legislature in the country. Given the immediate squalor surrounding them, these plutocrats are largely segregated from the general population of 49,000, which sports an average household income of just $25,000. Forty-four percent of its children live in poverty, and the murder rate has hit eight times the national average. For decades it's been an ever shrinking and increasingly dangerous remnant of a rust belt town.

Back at city hall, the clock had just struck 6:00. I was sitting in the back softly chatting with a few reporter friends.

The meeting began with a roll call by a city clerk who had difficulties reading the printed page. "Good evening everybody," then announced the President of City Council. "Thank you all for coming." But, given the dire state of the city, you'd think "you all" would encompass more than a couple dozen. But most quit caring long ago.

After roll call, a brief invocation and awkward moment of silence, everyone stood to address the flag. As always, the words "under God" were proudly emphasized. Everyone then settled in for a long night of committee reports and ordinance readings, with the understanding that none of it really mattered.

Over the decades, Harrisburg, Pennsylvania, had devolved into a city wrought with problems. Theoretically, those problems began in 1812 when it was chosen as the capital. City leaders waged a vigorous campaign to acquire the "honor," thinking it would balance the city's industrial reputation and provide a near recession-proof economy. Their mistake was assuming politicians from sophisticated cities such as Philadelphia and Pittsburgh would care. Instead of Harrisburg reaping the benefit of the state's hierarchy, it garnered their scorn. A mindset soon emerged where this small town was viewed as a second-class citizen, near useless land surrounding a massive state authority. After the railroads, steel and textile mills began to shut down in the 1950s that mentality expanded to include suburban lawmakers. Once Harrisburg was seen as a liability, it was essentially orphaned. State aristocrats mostly ignored the city and its people, unless they could control both. That precedent was set early on and repeated throughout the decades.

And Harrisburg couldn't defend itself. The city's government lacks the sophistication of its Commonwealth counterpart. With the exception of a full-time mayor, elected officials are otherwise part-time. City Council members, who have other lives and other jobs, or no jobs at all, carry out their scheduled meetings in the evenings. They have no staff and meager salaries. When it comes to education and experience, we're not talking Kennedy School degrees in public policy or urban planning. For some, we're not even talking degrees. The 21st Century and capital status notwithstanding, Harrisburg city government, like similar municipalities, are a throwback to Mayberry, USA except that Andy Griffin and Barney

Fife never had delusions of grandeur or lived beyond their means. At this point, Harrisburg couldn't even afford ink cartridges.

By the night of this particular Council meeting, Harrisburg was already broke. It gave up trying to pay its bills long ago, leading to a monumental financial collapse. It could barely even pay its workers. The city had so little money it couldn't even keep track of the money it didn't have. And the lawsuits were stacked higher than the pretentious brass man who stands atop the nearby Capitol dome.

Being broke was nothing new. The 'Burg had been for years. Even as it was thriving with new business, commerce and institutions a few years earlier, it was broke. The problem was very few people knew. And most of those unaware weren't interested in finding out—and that includes the media.

Aside from the elected officials who are required to attend, Council sessions are largely a destination for community regulars, along with those with nothing else to do and nowhere else to go. It also attracts the slightly deranged; whether that applies to the policy makers before those in attendance, is up for debate.

And this night appeared no different. To most, the crowd looked banal and familiar, except for the presence of a quirky-looking man in a loud pin-stripe suite with round tortoise-shell glasses and a briefcase. With his Einstein hair and seemingly commensurate wit, he looked necessarily out of place. But his importance would soon be known.

Though, while he appeared out of place, he wasn't so out of place. Council sessions are generally used by an array of folks as a platform to vent their frustrations. Under the faded lights of public access cameras, they rant mostly nonsense. Meanwhile their leaders sit perched on an elevated dais in front of tired walnut paneling. Alternately, they primp and posture for the media.

This open forum is what attracts the city's colorful. While entertaining, it's rarely newsworthy. Council regulars include folks like the jobless veteran who cries disability, while he drives a new Mustang and exercises regularly in local parks. There's also the robust white-bearded environmental lawyer who once worked for the Grateful Dead and never lost the look. There's the old, tiny homeless man in the black turban who, no matter the topic, bemoans racial inequalities. He's usually followed by the thin stutterer in the leather golf hat who demands bars shut down early and stop interrupting his sleep. On this particular evening, there was some sanity on the floor. One audience member implored Council to forget about the past and move forward with any financial recovery plan. Immediately after, Council was informed that Occupy Harrisburg was having a rally.

Also not missing from the meeting was Lewis Butts—a short, bizarre, bald man who had an infectious zeal for the city. This future mayoral candidate would campaign on the installation of web-based cameras in the chief executive's office so people could watch him via the free Wi-Fi he'd distribute throughout the impoverished city.

In tonight's epiphany he put forth the construction of a hydroelectric dam to span the listless Susquehanna River. He claimed a windfall of revenue. Apparently he didn't know the previous Mayor had already issued $300 million in debt back in the early 1980s for this very same pipe dream—a pipe dream he repeatedly refinanced. Yet, despite all that indebtedness, not one gallon of the river was ever dredged, nor was an ounce of mortar poured. Instead, the bond proceeds were reinvested to reap millions. Money the city could now desperately use, but none could be found.

Following public comment, the room slept through the committee reports. The night's biggest draw featured, "eliminating the requirement for property inspections unless the property being transferred is currently condemned." This and an ordinance to increase the parking tax were passed seven to zero. The media still had no headline. I had no lead. I shouldn't even have been there. But in a city this chaotic, everything must be covered.

As I inattentively sat in the back pondering my career choice, a fellow reporter who arrived a few minutes before me, mentioned something odd that happened earlier. Before Council meetings, it's customary for Council members to sit around a square table off to the side and cryptically whisper. These meetings are mandated to be held in public. But even for those seated nearby, the animated discussion could barely be heard, and rarely understood.

Yet, this reporter told me that during tonight's meeting, in a moment of unforeseen passion, the Council President, Gloria Martin-Roberts, suddenly lashed out at the strange white man in the tortoise-shell glasses. She threatened to have him forcibly removed from the building for simply responding to a question about why he was there. Roberts, he said, looked visibly agitated; her face had morphed into the same color as her deep purple blouse. The outburst was wildly out of character for the gracious and lovely African-American grandmother.

He said that outburst caught the attention of the media who then slowly began to circle the table. But he was highly skeptical as to the root of the frenzy. The fracas typified the fact that race and color remain a not-so-subtle dividing line. For centuries Harrisburg was controlled by the white GOP establishment. Now, it was run nearly exclusively by minority Democrats. At the time, there was only one elected white person in all of Harrisburg's Legislative and Executive branches. Rumors of reverse racism throughout the capital's government were not much challenged.

But my reporter friend said this energy seemed different given the current elevated levels of tension. Everyone was already on edge and prepared to fight. In many precincts all communication had long ceased. The state had recently attempted to impose a fiscal recovery plan onto the city. It was rejected by Council, who saw it as a canard. Frustrated at the hubris of the unsophisticated city Legislature, the state simply took over. A receiver—a first in state history—was appointed to replace Harrisburg's elected officials. In a town that's 75 percent minority, an old, unelected, white guy (who worked for a Wall Street firm) took control. The city's financial crisis morphed into a fight over self-governance, racial understanding and Constitutional interpretation.

It was now a full hour after the Council meeting began and the media still had nothing to call a lead. I texted the newsroom to tell them they may want to consider moving me to something else. But then around 7:00 everything changed. With no foreseeable or acceptable way out of the mess it had found itself in, City Council decided to take action—making the night of October 11, 2011, historic in not only Pennsylvania history, but American.

Suddenly, with few paying attention, one Council member issued a proposal to suspend chamber rules. The groggy eyes of onlookers drifted open as a "gang of four" emerged and quickly approved the motion. Light whispers shot through the audience. Yet, few knew what was really happening.

Without warning, the unknown man of unique character emerged from the crowd, briefcase by his side. With a lawyering confidence, he proclaimed his allegiance to Council. The President threatened to have him removed from the building. But her aggressive attempt to control the moment lacked true authority. When it was clear the votes were present, a clearly outmaneuvered Council President sighed: "You can't change the rules in the middle of the game!" Together, the "gang of four" ex-claimed: "That's what the state did!"

Energy levels intensified as the reporters and residents began to realize what was unfolding. America was about to change, and less than 50 people would witness it.

Amongst moans and cries from the audience, one Council member called for a vote. Another seconded it.

The room stood as Council took a stand. With a 4-3 majority, Harrisburg City Council openly defied the state and challenged Wall Street and the financial world by hiring a bankruptcy attorney.

Council had determined that bankruptcy was Harrisburg's best option to keep essential services and to claw back the millions paid to lawyers, consultants and Wall Street bankers. Council made a strong statement; it wanted control of its own future. But the Commonwealth sought power to conquer.

At 11:45 that night, the papers were filed in U.S. Federal Bankruptcy Court. Harrisburg had just become the first capital city in American history to seek Chapter 9 protection. Despite its uncertain outcome, the world would once again know the name, Harrisburg. This once-revered city had reclaimed its historical relevance.

Now, the race was on! With Council's courageous vote, this disabled town would be torn in three directions: Council was heading to bankruptcy court; the new Mayor was trying to matter by implementing her own recovery plan; meanwhile the state wanted total control.

For 28 years, Harrisburg's famous Mayor dined with the largest financial institutions in the world—enjoying grand and visible success. Money was the drug. And the lawyers, bankers and bond insurers carelessly peddled it—irrespective of the likely and familiar result.

Then, like true drug dealers when an overdose killed the client, Wall Street washed its hands of culpability. The firms wanted made whole and refused to offer concessions. Meanwhile, the impoverished city residents were expected to pay up. This created an "us" versus "them" battle: a broke, inexperienced and uneducated small-town elected body against the richest and most powerful institutions in the world.

The "us" part was a new City Council made up of part-time public servants. Most swept to office during the fall of the previous mayoral regime. They were largely moms, dads and grandparents who just loved their town and wanted to see it begin to heal. Some didn't have college degrees or even full-time jobs. They made $20,000 a year. But they had the courage to wage a war without the means to fund it. Despite massive pressure from the county, state and capital markets, they defended city residents by challenging the global elite and filing for Chapter 9 protection.

Adding to the impossible situation, many feared Pennsylvania's own Governor allied himself with Wall Street instead of the people. The city was defaulting on its debt, preferring to pay its workers over the big banks. But the Governor's chief of staff was from the law firm that represented the bond insurers—who wanted paid. It would later be discovered, that same law firm had lobbied Pennsylvania's General Assembly to pass a little-noticed amendment to a budget bill barring the city from filing for bankruptcy—which had the potential to deepen the bond insurers' (Wall Street's) loses.

By morning, the bankruptcy news had spread globally. Council, and its new lawyer, faced hordes of media converge. For foreign media long tired of the decline of the Euro, and various nation-states, Harrisburg was a welcome respite and a turning of the tables on western democracy. Al Jazeera wanted to know if this signaled the end of American capitalism. The Wall Street Journal questioned the bankruptcy lawyer's plan to battle the state. German newspapers couldn't understand how the city's debt was allowed to reach seven times its budget. Fox News, the BBC, CNN and all the networks suddenly became interested in Central Pennsylvania politics. But what few realized was this was not the end. Nor was it the beginning. It was simply a story that hadn't been told.

2: HONING A HERITAGE

DURING THE CLOSING MONTHS of 2010, Pennsylvania elected a new Republican governor, Joe Paterno earned his 400th career win at Penn State, and I arrived in Harrisburg for work. In the weeks leading up to my move from Madison, Wisconsin, I had heard so much about the city, I thought it was quite the unique place. And there was plenty of evidence to support this belief; much of it centered on the city's chief executives, former Mayor Stephen Reed and his successor Linda Thompson, who had been sworn in nine months before my arrival.

Thompson was the capital's first female and first black Mayor. A Howard University graduate, she purported to have obtained a degree in communications. But her college and job experience notwithstanding, she fit in more with the city's desperate underclass. The youngest daughter in a large family, she herself had a child while in high school. Early in her term, that child was arrested for attempted rape. Later in her term, her brother was arrested for theft and witness intimidation. In court, his victim accused Thompson of receiving what was stolen. Another one of her brothers spent 28 years in jail for murder. Then, there was that nagging question of the non-profit she founded called "Love Ship." To this day, many question what it actually accomplished—outside of collecting donations.

When it came to her style of governance, she repeatedly claimed that only the Almighty was her true counselor. This was most apparent during her public three-day religious fast and prayer. She had concluded the answers to Harrisburg's problems could not be found in mere humans, only God. Her public display encouraged Current TV commentator, Keith Olbermann, to place her on his "worst persons" list. He opined following her fast, "Remarkably, it didn't simply rain dollar bills." Thompson responded, "It could have been worse. Keith might have contributed to my campaign." She then promised to keep Olbermann in her prayers saying, "You never know, [his] ratings might improve."

With her clumpy mascara, librarian glasses and endless hair extensions, Thompson created an easy caricature of herself. But it was her outstanding quotes and even more outstanding actions that caused many to rub their heads in disbelief. Yet, somehow she did succeed in dethroning a king who held the reigns of the city for nearly three decades. But given the financial collapse she inherited, many believe Mayor Stephen Reed simply retired without formally doing so.

During my first few days on the job, everyone warned me about Mayor Thompson. When I finally met her I learned why. Over the years and throughout the financial collapse, the Mayor and I developed a very contemptuous relationship. Despite hundreds of encounters, I was the only reporter she refused to acknowledge by name. During press conferences she referred to every other reporter by name. I was simply know as, "you." I figured it was her way of letting me know where we stood.

As unique an image as Thompson created for the city, I learned that the elongated story of Harrisburg is not at all unique. It's the story of America. You may not realize, but you already know its history. It was taught to you in

school and through the many legends passed down
through the generations. You're familiar with the area's
origins and how it developed. You're accustomed to the
way European settlers treated the native population and
exploited the land. You understand how it harvested and
produced raw material and then shipped it on steel rails
or by boat. Your childhood text books contained chapters
on the impact of the Industrial Revolution and The Civil
War. The names may be different, but the anecdotes are
the same.

No matter the morality or magnificence, Harrisburg
and America are linked in a way whereas went one so
went the other. This reality is not by chance, but rather
by necessity. They share a rare heritage that started long
before they even existed by name. And that heritage
allows them limited mutual exclusivity. Throughout the
decades and centuries, the two seemed to move in
tandem. We can only hope they are tethered no more.

Does the following sound familiar?

Central Pennsylvania was settled by Native Americans
thousands of years before the first Europeans. Existing
animal trails and the river offered easy transportation.
The soil was some of the nation's most fertile. When the
settlers arrived, they quickly realized the terrain's advantages.

Soon, the Native Americans were seen as only an
annoyance. The Paxton Boys, a vigilante group of
Presbyterian Scots-Irishmen, assembled to handle the
problem. In December of 1763, the Paxtons massacred a
group of Susquehannock Indians and then burned the
cabin where the bodies lay in pieces. They didn't stop
until every member of the tribe was killed, and with it the
language and culture. No one was ever arrested for the
killings (U-S-History).

Like others of a similar ilk, the Paxton Boys' efforts
were not forgotten. Within the Harrisburg area, multiple
churches, a heavily trafficked street, and even a
municipality share the name. But it can also be said the

Susquehannock were not forgotten. The longest waterway on the east coast, which cuts through Harrisburg, bears the name, Susquehanna River.

Harrisburg's location and access to raw material allowed it to quickly thrive as a producer of raw material. With the Native Americans out of the way, it soon solidified its position as a business center for east-west, north-south trade. Steel and iron became the dominant industries that fattened a gluttonous nation. The region attracted ambitious immigrants from around the globe, who melted into their surroundings. Pictures of this time depict a thriving city of soot.

Massive railroads, including the Pennsylvania and Reading (as seen on a Monopoly board), merged in the city. The Harrisburg Cotton Factory, Bethlehem Steel, Central Iron Works, Lochiel Rolling Mill, Pennsylvania Steel Company and Pennsylvania Steel Works were just some of the companies that helped forge one of the most industrialized cities in the northeastern United States.

With the influx of industrial capital and the half-mile wide Susquehanna River, the city became an early leader of modern bridge construction. Whether by stone, steel or concrete, Charles Dickens took notice. During a trip to the city he called the bridges and scenery, "bold and striking" (Dickens).

The area also built a strong reputation as an important stop along the Underground Railroad. Legend has it militant abolitionist John Brown acquired the money, supplies and ammunition he used at Harper's Ferry in Harrisburg (Scott).

"We were last night confronted by a most brutal and disgraceful mob. To the everlasting shame, and infamy of the people of Harrisburg," wrote Frederick Douglass to his friend Sydney Gay after visiting the city in 1847. The fervent abolitionist movement in central PA inspired Douglass' trip. But the stones, eggs and firecrackers thrown at him as he addressed a crowd at the courthouse may have soured his fondness for the area. "The atrocious character of the proceedings is sufficiently palpable, and Harrisburg one day will be ashamed of it," he later wrote to the New York Tribune (Douglass).

It's hard to believe now, but Harrisburg once held such influence that in December of 1839 the Whig Party held its national convention at the Zion Lutheran Church on Fourth Street and nominated William Henry Harrison. Harrison would later be elected the nation's ninth president. To this day, Harrisburg is the smallest city to ever host a major, national political convention—a prestigious title it's unlikely to ever relinquish.

The city was so meaningful to American life that Confederate General Robert E. Lee perhaps bestowed upon Harrisburg its greatest praise. By the 1860s, Harrisburg had emerged as the heart of the North. Like veins stretching across the countryside, its rails pumped the blood that kept the Union viable—allowing the Atlantic Coast direct access to the Midwest. Exploiting this advantage, the Union established its largest training center near the banks of the Susquehanna. From 1861 to 1865, more than 300,000 troops passed through Camp Curtin.

General Lee knew the Union could not survive without its rails, which is why the Army of Northern Virginia twice targeted Harrisburg for invasion. The first attempt ended in 1862 following the Battle of Antietam (Gillespie). That day, September 17, remains the deadliest 24-hours in American military history—23,000 men were killed, wounded or went missing.

General Lee's second attempt to capture Harrisburg resulted in the bloodiest *battle* in American history (Wingert). Had Lee defeated Meade and advanced to Harrisburg, the war may have been effectively over. Without the rails to connect the north, the Union would have slowly suffocated. But as Lee marched his massive army north he was stopped in Gettysburg, which stole the historical glory many feel was rightfully Harrisburg's.

In 1861, while en-route to Washington for his inauguration, Abraham Lincoln briefly stepped off his train to address a Harrisburg crowd saying, "While I am exceedingly gratified to see the manifestation upon your streets of your military force here... I do most sincerely hope that we shall have no use for them" (Nicolay).

Four years later, President Lincoln would return to Harrisburg on another train—the one carrying his casket. On April 21, 1865, he lay in state in the Pennsylvania House of Representatives.

Harrisburg's vital role in the Civil War goes largely unmentioned in the history books. Against the backdrop of Gettysburg, Antietam, Vicksburg, Sherman, Grant and Lee, it's understandable. So, like most people, you can imagine my surprise when I first learned the National Civil War Museum is located here. But following my first encounter with Mayor Stephen Reed, it made much more sense.

As much as people bemoaned the election of Mayor Thompson, they lauded the tenure of Mayor Reed. In 1982, Reed was elected and took over a city that had lost nearly a quarter of its population in the previous decade. And that quarter consisted of those who had the resources to leave. And with them, they took their tax revenue. It was rumored an outgoing city official left Reed bankruptcy papers on his desk.

Yet, despite the obvious problems he encountered, by the early 2000s the city's remarkable turnaround earned Reed the title of "Pennsylvania's most popular and successful mayor" by The PA Report. His achievements were even internationally recognized. In 2006, the City Mayors organization named Reed the third best mayor in the world—and the best in America.

Mayor Reed was a homegrown boy who made a name for himself as a member of Harrisburg River Rescue. Every other day he was in the media for pulling someone out of the Susquehanna River and saving their lives. At 25-years-old, the young Democrat won a seat in the State Legislature. Bright, but not necessarily an intellectual, he was clean-cut and sure of himself, genuinely likeable with an enjoyable confidence. Despite the large crowds he attracted, he had a way to make you feel like the only person in the room. He was the prototype for the 24-hour-a-day, hands-on big-city mayor.

His inauguration at 32 proved to be more of a coronation. It's a post he gripped in a strangle hold for the next 28 years. During five of his re-election cam-paigns he was endorsed by both political parties. He created an environment where if you weren't his cheer-leader, you were his enemy. He not only controlled the city, its police and fire services, but also the schools, media and entire economy—both above and (some would argue) below ground. Believe me, I know this sounds incredulous. Before I fully understood, I didn't want to believe one man could acquire such dictatorial powers in America. But it happened. Reed controlled the region through fear. Little was possible financially or politically without his blessing.

Given the god-like aura surrounding Mayor Reed, you can imagine I was a bit nervous when I first met him. It was fitting our inaugural interview would take place at the crowning achievement of his political career, the National Civil War Museum.

Located on top of a hill resembling Little Round Top, it featured architecture similar to that found in Wash-ington, D.C.'s museums. The National Civil War Museum is indeed impressive. But with only 40,000 visitors a year, it's hard to consider it a success. Had it not been located just 38 miles northeast of Gettysburg and in a very depressed part of the city, it may have done better. But that was all part of Mayor Reed's plan.

By the time I had met Reed, he had been out of office for a year. The city had not yet fully collapsed, but it was having trouble. Many just assumed the issues were caused by his incompetent successor and petulant City Council. It was the 10th anniversary of the museum. Reed accepted an invitation to speak. It amounted to his first public appearance since leaving office.

Outside the conference room, I stood with every media outlet in the area. Radio, TV, print, we were all there.

With the soft lighting, established row of tripods and feel of the moment, you'd have thought a Hollywood star would soon emerge from the elevator.

I could tell the media was a little uneasy in waiting. Reed still held tremendous power. Of all the reporters there, I was the newest and by far the most naïve. I had seen pictures of the man before, but wasn't really sure what to expect.

Forgoing the elevator, Reed took the steps. Using his umbrella as a cane, he arduously made his way up. He appeared to struggle, but his pride forbade him to show it. He looked frail and tired—his body worn with a slight hunch in his back. His face drew a pale fatigue. In his loafers, he may have come up to my shoulder. As I said, I wasn't sure what to expect. But this certainly was not it.

Yet, when he stepped up to the camera lights, his back arched with a relaxed energy. As he prepared to perform, his umbrella became just an umbrella. During the interview, Reed refused to discuss the issues surrounding Mayor Thompson. It was not yet one year into her administration and protests to remove her from that post had become commonplace. The entire city seemed to be mourning Reed's stunning electoral loss.

One reporter asked Reed how he was able to revive the city when most everyone thought it was an impossible task. He responded by speaking of his legacy. With a unique combination of pride and humility, he discussed his ability to create "institutions." His words came easily. His eyes appeared honest. He said once you create one institution others will follow.

No one in the media argued. We just nodded in obvious agreement. You see, when Reed was elected, the city had few if any sustainable or viable institutions. During his seven terms, his leadership led to the creation of Harrisburg University of Science and Technology, the Harrisburg Senators (double AA affiliate of the Washington Nationals), The Pennsylvania National Fire Museum, Whitaker Center for Science and the Arts, the beautiful downtown Hilton, the recreational City Island and Civil War Museum—just to name a few. It was estimated more than $4 billion of private sector investments poured into the city during his time and property values increased 800 percent.

During the interview, he called that "the legacy of my era" which will last for generations. I asked him if he thought more institutions could be added given the current administration's early shortcomings.

"Right now, I'm sorry to say the environment really isn't conducive to new initiatives in Harrisburg," Reed told me. "We will make sure the ones that already exist are sustained and that includes the National Civil War Museum."

That night, Reed delivered a resounding speech commemorating the museum's first decade. As he addressed the crowd, he no longer appeared frail or weak. He stood strong and honed an influential voice. With only 40,000 visitors a year, the museum was struggling. Rumor had it that it could shut down. But his words made me a believer in its future. At that moment, watching him speak, I began to understand his royal appeal. And it made me highly skeptical—and rapt with intrigue. I needed to know more—much more.

That night, as Reed said his goodbyes to the crowd, I was able to introduce myself. With so many attendees seeking his attention, our conversation was pleasantly brief. Though, it did serve the greater journalistic purpose of establishing a connection with the local elite. Towards the end of our encounter, I alluded to my love of American history. He suggested I tour the museum. "It's quite spectacular," he stated proudly. "You should take a Saturday afternoon and walk around." Despite the founder's personal invitation, to this day, I still have not done so. And I'm not entirely sure why.

A few months following my first encounter with Reed, the city fiscally imploded. Amongst the chaos, he somehow managed to avoid the spotlight. It would be a full 18 months before Reed and I would meet again. However, that encounter would not be so amicable.

3: THE MAKING OF A "MINIATURE PARIS"

PRIL 22, 2012 WAS A GOOD DAY for me. The prior year had been emotionally draining. My professional life, at that point, consisted of Harrisburg's financial crisis and Penn State's Jerry Sandusky crisis. If I wasn't covering yet another press conference about the city's dismal future or talking to a victim of its broken leadership, I was somewhere in Happy Valley interviewing the highly depressed. It wasn't a good year for Pennsylvania.

But on April 22, I got a break—a bit of good news; gasoline had just fallen below $4 a gallon. As an investigative reporter, I usually despise these types of stories. For my entire career, I've always argued against filling air time with the obvious. And for my entire career, management has overruled me. I just never understood why television reporters have to stand in snow to tell people at home it's snowing. If substantive information exists to accompany that weather shot, then the importance of the location is obvious. But more often than not, I see reporters standing in snow simply to stand in snow.

The same reasoning applies to gas prices. Most everyone who drives buys gas. They know what the price

29

is. Why does a reporter have to tell them? Yet, on this particular day, I suspended that fight—much to the shock of my coworkers. Actually, looking back, it seems odd to celebrate gas prices of $3.99 a gallon. But I was more than happy to spin it.

After my photographer and I circled a few gas pumps questioning locals, we returned to the station. I wrote the story. He edited it. Then we found a gas station for our 10:00 and 11:00 live shots. All was right with the world. I should have known better.

As my photographer set up the lighting, a light rain began to fall. So, we simply set up under the convenience store's overhanging roof. When a sudden wind started throwing around the heavier rain, we moved to the building's shielded side. But when my phone began to ring, I just knew there'd be no easy adjustment.

"What?" I answered the phone already frustrated.

"We need you to check something out in Allison Hill." By its very nature, most reporters and photojournalists find the assignment desk annoying (a sentiment that is likely mutual). It exists to tell us what to do irrespective of the progress of our current assignment. It's very frustrating. When that number would appear on my phone, I invariably anticipated bad news.

"I have no interest in going to the ghetto," I asserted. "We have the lead story. Can't you send someone else?"

"You're the closest."

I probably sounded more uninterested than I realized. "What is it?"

"A house collapsed on a family. The scanners said kids may be trapped inside."

My hope for a less depressing day was over.

By the time we arrived on scene, a soaking rain had taken hold. It was about 9:45 at night. The absent moon, stuck behind clouds, provided little light. The road was closed, but we were allowed to park just a few dilapidated houses away, behind a ladder truck. Crews had the small house lit like a stadium. I grabbed an umbrella and begrudgingly opened the door.

My photographer stayed by the truck to get a few establishing shots. I walked towards the collapsed row home to see who was available to talk.

"The chief's not on scene," one fireman told me, the cold April rain streamed off his hard hat. The roar of the fire engines and the water splattering off them made it hard to hear. "We'll send out a presser before morning."

"Can you tell me anything?" My umbrella only kept my top half dry. I could feel the water creeping up my pants and socks. My skin tightened.

"Sorry, man," he replied. "Not authorized. But the family is over there." He pointed across the street to a couple adults and a slew of children crammed onto a rickety porch. My photographer was now by the house getting close-ups, which were impressive. The roof had collapsed through the third floor and onto the second. The abandoned row home next to it lay on top. It appeared the latter caused the former. How someone wasn't killed, I'll never know.

"Excuse me, I'm sorry to bother you." I approached the porch with caution. Everyone responds to media differently. "Are any of you the occupants of that home?"

A forlorn, white stump of a lady approached me. "I rent it." She looked like hell.

"I'm sorry to see what happened." And I really was. How awful. "Do you mind if I ask you a few questions for the news tonight?"

She nodded. I waved for my photographer. We didn't have much time. Camera rain gear only lasts so long.

"How many people lived in that house?" I asked as we waited.

"Eight!"

My eyes widened.

"Eight in *that* home?" I didn't intend for my surprise to be so obvious.

"Yeah, but no one was hurt." She didn't seem to think her circumstance was too peculiar. "We were lucky."

"Let's go out into the street," she walked down the steps and into the rain before I could stop her.

"Don't you want to stay under the roof?" I asked in bewilderment.

She softly shook her head. "My kids don't need to hear this."

I took a step towards her. "Well, at least come under my umbrella."

"I'm good." She shied away from my advance. "I can't get any colder or wetter. Keep yourself dry." The rain was hitting her so hard I couldn't tell if she were crying.

With her in a raggedy, oversized, drenched t-shirt, and me in a $600 suit protected by a station-issued umbrella, I interviewed the woman in that cold April shower. I had never felt so baseless.

She told me how her home had been falling apart for years. And the landlord refused to fix it. When it rained, it leaked. During winter, they lived in the cold. During summer, they lived in the heat.

On numerous occasions, she complained to the city about not only the condition of her home, but the abandoned structures around her. But nothing was done. Her calls were never even returned.

Harrisburg had a very well-publicized problem with blighted structures and equally as publicized lack of money to deal with it. This woman's house, and those around it, were probably on some list, somewhere. But attention was likely years away—if ever. Now, this entire family of eight had no place to stay. And the fault was not their own. As tenants, they were expected to pay their rent, which they did. In return, they expected a safe home in which to live. They didn't get it.

"It's horrible because I'm outside with my kids in the rain and I don't know what the next step is going to be. I knew this would happen. The city should tear down or fix up the houses, or the landlords, and not let them fall apart so the people suffer," she sobbed. I was pretty certain the lines under her eyes were tears and not rain.

After the interview, as is standard procedure, my photographer backed off to get some shots of her and I talking. It's the magic of TV. She went on to tell me her house was more than 100 years old and the inside was gorgeous. The wood work and the craftsmanship were just remarkable, she said. And judging by the ornate architecture of the surrounding homes, it was obvious this was once a prominent neighborhood.

Since Harrisburg's earliest days, its residents seemed to lack a certain hometown pride many American towns enjoyed. Few had praise for what the city had achieved during its first few centuries. But by the early 20th century, that mentality began to change. Ambitious entrepreneurs and factory owners realized the area's potential and developed a plan to realize it. Harrisburg no longer had to settle for being just another small industrial town on the banks of a river. Like Pittsburgh and Philadelphia, it could be refined with colorful culture and competitive sport, while retaining that certain communal feel larger towns lack (Beers).

The idea of a grand city was quickly accepted. Harrisburg began to view itself as a reflection of the Commonwealth cast in its own unique identity. It had become one of the nation's leading industrial cities. Now it was time for more.

By 1900, poverty in the city was hard to find, as were the unemployed. Its middle class neighborhoods were built and manicured by the same hands that crafted steel and wove textiles. Handsome brick and black shuttered homes couldn't go up fast enough. From 1850 to 1900 the number of residents increased from 7,000 to 50,000 (which proved higher than its population 110 years later in 2010). In the coming decades, that number would nearly double, again. And those moving to the Susquehanna Valley were learned, skilled and motivated.

As the city was going through this change in thought, so was state government. Pennsylvania, at the time, was populated with heavily conservative, small government-minded folks. But their politicians also wanted more. Starting around 1900, the Capitol complex embarked on a massive expansion project. At the turn of the 20th century, the Capitol had 300 employees. Two short decades later, that ballooned to 1,400—all with barely a "big government Democrat" in sight (Beers). For these new aristocrats, the current industrial city was simply unsuitable. Crowded in dirt and smoke, the ruling class demanded a town worthy of their stature.

The spark for the state government movement came in February of 1897 when the state house burned down. That Capitol was a reflection of the modest mindset of early Pennsylvanians. Federalist in styling with a red brick structure, it cost only $244,000 ($3.3 million in 2015 money). But its burning provided an opening for state government to bloat. The new Capitol, completed in 1906, cost $14 million ($390 million in 2015 money). It was so magnificent, all the murals and sculptures took three decades to complete.

At 520 feet long, 272 feet tall with 630,000 square feet of Renaissance revival, it was spectacularly unnecessary. It has 60 more rooms than the United States Capitol in Washington, DC. The dome towering above the marble imperial staircase is modeled after St. Peter's Cathedral in Rome. With Beaux-Arts themes, it's simply the most incredible state building in America—nearly $400 million of marble, granite, stained glass, brass, bronze and mosaics. It's truly a magnificent symbol of political indulgence.

At its dedication, President Theodore Roosevelt christened it, "the handsomest building I ever saw." For its commemoration, the rails ran additional trains to accommodate the captivated crowds.

Like many swollen government projects, the Capitol construction was not without its fraud. Five people, including the Capitol's architect, served two years in jail for drastically overpaying suppliers. Only a clever novelist could have offered such a unique foreshadowing for how Harrisburg—100 years later—would recklessly manage its own finances.

With all the spending, state government emerged as the city's largest industry. Pennsylvania's Republicans had created a massive centralized government—bigger than California, Illinois and New York. They were so successful at solidifying their rule; their beloved Capitol soon grew too small. The black neighborhood of the Eighth Ward would bear this load, as the state took it over (yet another peculiar foreshadowing). With the additional 541 properties, the Capitol grounds expanded to 45 acres.

Nevertheless, the city now had an extravagant Capitol filled with pretentious nobles who gawked at the unrefined real-estate that surrounded them. Something had to be done. The natural surroundings with the river, mountains and valleys provided a strong base. Now, the remainder would have to be built.

In 1902, Harrisburg welcomed a new Mayor, Vance McCormick. The All-American quarterback from Yale won office touting an ambitious City Beautiful Movement. With millions being spent, powerful families such as Cameron and McCormick emerged as philanthropists. Other wealthy families attracted by the area built mansions along Front Street overlooking the Susquehanna's cut through the Appalachian chain.

Harrisburg's aspirations reached beyond the local scene; its achievements had global implications. As an early leader in electricity, it was the second city in America with electrified trolleys. It already claimed to have the world's first lighted church, a feat Thomas Edison himself witnessed (Beers).

It sounds odd now, but if Harrisburg wanted to be sophisticated it needed a state-of-the-art sanitation system. So a project with intercepting sewer and flood controls was designed. A $2,500,000 water treatment facility was built in 1905 to supply the city with pure, filtered water—a rarity of the day.

The beautification movement also meant a move toward worldly arts. The centerpiece of which was the Grand Opera House that seated 1,324 and hosted acts like Houdini. Complete with an orchestra and peanut gallery, it was stunning. The arts were so big, the city produced Tony Award winners, such as Donald Oenslager, and writers like Helen Reimensynder who penned 35 novels. Jack Dempsey and Joe Louis refereed fights in the city (Beers).

The wide Susquehanna River challenged architects to span it in increasingly impressive ways. The Rockville Bridge at 3,820 feet long is said to be the world's longest stone-arch railroad span. And that bridge is still in use.

With a highly educated population came a strong demand for news. It made sense Harrisburg would produce the nation's first state house press corps, founded near the turn of the century (Beers).

For all of the City Beautiful Movement's achievements, its sponsors most celebrated the creation of a natural park system, which encircled the city. The "Green Belt" is 19 miles of trails and gardens. By the end of the movement, Harrisburg achieved more parks per square mile and per resident than any other American city.

Mayor Edward Gross proclaimed in the first decade of the 20th century that Harrisburg was "the most prosperous and hustling city of its size in the country" (Kelker). Few Harrisburgers would disagree.

The City Beautiful Movement lasted 30 years, inspiring American Civil Association president J. Horace McFarland to proclaim, "No other city in all this broad land has done all these things concurrently, harmoniously, and entirely upon the plans of experts" (Wilson).

Unlike the scandal surrounding the construction of the Capitol, there was no sign of corruption during Harrisburg's big expanse, which may explain its success.

The improvements which totaled about $26 million in loans were said to have paid for themselves in increased valuation.

Wrote respected Harrisburg newspaper reporter, Paul Beers: "By 1920 Harrisburg was a prosperous contemporary city, far beyond the wildest hallucinations of its most visionary citizens just 30 years before. Never again would so much growth take place, and never before had Harrisburg been so awakened."

In 1930, Bell Telephone massively increased service to Harrisburg estimating the city's population would soon hit 200,000. But it never even got close.

Unfortunately, much like the woman's house that collapsed in the cold April rain, many of the City Beautiful Movement's achievements discussed in this chapter no longer exist.

4: THE HARRISBURG HAUGHTY

TO REFER TO SOMETHING AS "unprecedented" is to say it's never before happened. Along with infamous, ironic and literally, it's one of the most misused terms in the English language. But, I think it's safe in saying what happened in Harrisburg on February 14, 2011, was indeed unprecedented.

It was Valentine's Day, and Linda Thompson had been Mayor for about a year. And in that short time, a serious case of voter's remorse had already set in. She had succeeded in alienating the area's gays by calling the city Controller a "homosexual, evil little man." She alienated many whites when she fired a successful white school superintendent to hire a less qualified black one. That move later alienated the fiscal conservatives when the white superintendent sued for wrongful termination and was awarded $2.4 million.

While at a packed town hall meeting concerning a severe spike in crime, she alienated very worried middle class homeowners by arrogantly proclaiming, "I want you to know that I am in control of this ship." A short time later, she alienated the non-believers by stating emphatically, "I am no bankruptcy attorney, but I am a

praying woman. Only God can fix the financial mess of
the city." She'd further alienate those same voters by
repeatedly announcing, "I tell God every day that I'm
honored he chose me to be the head of this city."

Early in her term, when the Mayor and certain Council
members were together, they would chant in unison, "You
go sister. You go girl." But sisterhood notwithstanding, a
deep schism was developing given the city's finances and
the Mayor's incomprehensible coziness with Republican
Governor Tom Corbett. Soon, the relationship between
City Council and the Mayor would collapse along with the
city. Communication between Harrisburg's legislative and
executive branches would soon exist only through the
media.

When the spotlight inevitably fell upon Mayor Thompson's incompetence and elitism, she did nothing to help
herself. A local film maker recorded (and then circulated)
video of her loading her entourage into a black, city-
owned Tahoe only to drive across the street from city hall
to the Hilton to attend a conference.

Within months of her leadership, dozens of city
employees quit. She cycled through communications
directors so regularly, I never knew who to call. It wasn't
uncommon for the current spokesman to have the voice-
mail recording of the previous.

Mayor Thompson projected a harsh, unwavering and
overbearing image—at a time when Harrisburg desperately craved unification. The capital needed capital,
investment and the help of the surrounding municipalities. But, she made no visible attempt to court any of
them. Life was crumbling all around her. Yet, instead of
focusing on the problems within, she lamented the media
for portraying her as an "angry, black woman in power."
And what happened on that frigid Monday afternoon in
February, didn't alter those portrayals.

Frustration over Mayor Thompson convinced about
250 mid-staters to organize a Valentine's Day rally. The
march to "Restore Sanity to Harrisburg" was intended to

force her resignation. Since the city doesn't have a provision to recall a mayor, this was their only chance.

The crowd was more diverse than the city itself. And their reasons for being there were equally as diverse.

"We don't need that in a city that's in crisis," stated a self-proclaimed gay man concerning her callous comments about the Controller.

Another man added, "If many of us in our own offices or at our jobs would have said the things she said, we would be fired."

"I don't know what would happen if she resigned, but I'd find it hard to believe it could be any worse," one Harrisburg man told the local paper (PennLive).

Another man showed up to object to Thompson's public injections of faith. "By making decisions [rooted in God] as an elected official, I feel she directly puts citizens at risk."

The former president of the Greater Harrisburg Branch of the NAACP even showed up to protest the city's first black mayor with a sign that read, "Linda, Lead or Leave." She told local media, "Leadership means you have to stop fighting all the time—with your own staff, at least."

The protesters assembled below the Mayor's second-story city hall window chanting and holding signs that read in part: "God told me our mayor is insane" and "This homosexual evil little man wants you out of office."

Then, to the amazement of the crowd (and the media), halfway through the boisterous rally, Thompson, dressed in bright red with shiny yellow jewels, appeared at her office window. With every media outlet in the area recording below, Thompson taunted the crowd by using both hands to gesture "thumbs up" and "thumps down." All the while mouthing, "I'm staying." She then held her hands in a prayerful position and bowed. The crowd came unglued.

With the Mayor bent at the waist, deep boos echoed through the city. These were soon followed with chants of "We want you out. We want you out." Thompson remained at the window, refusing to retreat. The pithier chant of "Get out. Get out" quickly emerged. Police slowly encircled the crowd as it grew in size and intensity.

With the Mayor now smiling and clapping, a protester hiding in the back packed a snowball and launched it. Flung with great force, the white sphere sailed through the air with a definite purpose. The protesters erupted in cheer as that little orb of frozen water neared its target. The Mayor never saw it coming. The anticipation was overwhelming. Not in a long time had Harrisburgers been so excited—or had so much to cheer about.

When that white ball exploded against her office window, the startled Mayor jolted backwards. With the glass recoiling, her jagged finger commanded an officer to find the thrower. She then re-approached the window—this time with her hand up, in a princess wave. A pageant-like smile enveloped her face.

"I'm staying," she mouthed again—her princess wave obnoxiously slowed. She then blew a kiss as her aides slowly closed the blinds. Like a Broadway performer delivering her final act, the curtain closed. She was gone. The highly annoyed crowd eventually dispersed. It was media gold.

In our dozens, if not hundreds of encounters, I got the impression that Mayor Thompson desperately wanted to be city royalty. Unfortunately, she was 85 years too late. You see, before Harrisburg provided the impetus for books on financial disasters, novelists were attracted to the city by its romanticism.

"[In Harrisburg] social life was more active than that of cities of comparable size, and this produced a social manner that would have been usually encountered in much larger cities."

John O'Hara penned those words in his 1960 novel *Ourselves to Know*. It was also in this novel that the heroine referred to Harrisburg as a "miniature Paris..." with its "substantial Capitol... the wide, tree-lined residential streets; the shops, where she was called madam;

the hotels, busy and ornate and with music always in the background..."

O'Hara grew up near the Yuengling Brewery in Pottsville, but moved to Harrisburg to more accurately capture the city's essence. His sprawling admiration for the town led to more books featuring Pennsylvania's capital. Hollywood found the town so enchanting; his 1949 novel *A Rage to Live* became a movie, starring Suzanne Pleshette. It opened in 1965.

During the first half of the 20th Century, Harrisburgers bought into the city's greatness. This feeling of political and civil superiority was rooted in a solid list of accomplishments. The capital city believed it was simply better. And for a while, it probably was.

This City Beautiful Movement started as a simple idea to improve urban life. But it quickly morphed into an ethos of hardline elitism. Eventually, it wasn't enough to simply evoke envy via natural parks, theaters and an advanced sewer system. Now, Harrisburg sought a suitable conduit to flaunt its newfound ego.

Wrote O'Hara in his novel: "Ahead of its time, compared to other cities of equal size, [Harrisburg] went in for a metropolitan social life." Where a socialite woman would wear a "sealskin cloak over a simple black taffeta gown, and her only jewelry was a thin diamond necklace."

As O'Hara depicted, the answer to Harrisburg's problem lay in a lack of social clubs. But similar to the City Beautiful Movement, if residents wanted such a pristine social order, it would have to be built. And it was.

"The debut of the Harrisburg Club was one of the dazzling moments in local history. Some 400 plutocrats assembled, to be served by attendants dressed in livery of dark blue and gold braid," explained local newsman Paul Beers in his Harrisburg book *City Contented, City Discontented*.

The Harrisburg Club was designed to attract the city's "best blood"—where "plutocrats" could dine on the best foods, walk on the best hardwoods and breathe the best air. It was a place where ice was reportedly "served in the shape of a law book lettered in gold, while the menu was presented as a miniature legal document" (Beers). Here, society's most esteemed could mingle amongst equals. Only in placing orders, would they be lowered to conversing with a commoner.

"[The Club had] families who by custom get things without even asking for them, because the people of [Harrisburg] acknowledged some kind of superiority." John O'Hara could snark at the scene in his novels. Though, he was known to frequent the Club when away from his typewriter (Beers).

Club life in Harrisburg excelled via demand. People didn't relocate to central Pennsylvania to remain unnamed. Soon, the Harrisburg Club was accompanied by The Harrisburg Country Club—where Wild Bill Hickok was known to place bets with local politicians and industrial barons (Beers). Then, in 1904, the Elks opened a lodge followed by a Zembo Temple that same year.

Yet beyond the clubs and all the improvements, nothing in Harrisburg screamed "success" quite like the elegant $2.5 million Penn Harris Hotel. It opened in 1919 with 12 brick stories and 400 elegant rooms. With telephones and a bathtub in each suite, it was New York City in central Pennsylvania.

"If anybody ever tells me [Harrisburg's] a hick town—they won't be able to tell me that again. This is practically the Waldorf-Astoria," wrote O'Hara concerning the Penn Harris.

And if lounging in clubs and a world-class hotel still wasn't enough, Harrisburgers could always rub their library in the faces of the non-believers. At a time when the elite displayed books in their homes like trophies, education meant prestige. The Harrisburg Library opened in 1914 with a colonial limestone exterior and 10,000 books—more than most American universities at the time.

Urban life grew so grand; Harrisburg voluntarily opted for isolation. News from the outside was ignored. A fictional newspaper columnist in *A Rage to Live* detailed this self-absorption: "If the telegraph wire said 1000 people had been killed in an earthquake in Chile, the important news in [Harrisburg] would still be that a rich and beautiful young girl was going to go to be with a handsome, more or less unknown city slicker. It's regrettable, out of proportion, but it's true."

This rare romanticism attracted other novelists to use the city as a backdrop. Pulitzer Prize winner Conrad Richter featured the Harrisburg region in 1953's *The Light in the Forest*. James Boyd referred to the city's obsession with itself as a "narrow iron shell of life" in his 1936 release, *Roll River (Beers)*.

Harrisburg was indeed a marvelous place. For a smaller city, it had everything the larger city's had—but with convenience. Residency was so cherished the boundaries of city proper were purposefully limited so not to bestow it on the undeserving.

During the early 20th century, Harrisburg was the place to be and the place to be seen. It housed as much as 50 percent of the county's population. Yet incredibly, just a few decades later, what was half became a sixth.

In 1918, in honor of the city's achievements, the Navy commissioned the USS Harrisburg to serve in World War I. During the last two years of the war, this 560 foot auxiliary cruiser, made four voyages across the Atlantic supplying troops on the battlefields. The naming of this ship confirmed the belief of its residents that Harrisburg, indeed, held its own preeminence.

The City Beautiful Movement officially ended in the late 1920s. The USS Harrisburg was scrapped shortly before.

5: THE COLLAPSE

WHEN I FIRST ARRIVED in Harrisburg for work, my reporting focused on the present crisis. But as I talked to people and gathered knowledge, it seemed the bigger story wasn't what *was* happening, but rather *how* it happened.

When Mayor Thompson was elected, she inherited a city with a $50 million budget and nearly $300 million in debt. That made absolutely no sense to me. Didn't anyone think to stop accruing debt after $100 million? How about $200 million? All the while the man in charge keeps getting elected for 28 years and is considered one of the best mayors in the world? It made my head hurt.

I desperately needed answers. And my first came by way of a mostly forgotten City Council meeting from November 5, 2003. That night, City Council took a vote that many consider the beginning of the end. At that moment, years of financial tricks would finally catch up with Harrisburg.

After learning of this 2003 vote, I pulled the audio. I didn't know if there was a story there. I was more curious than anything. But when I got the CD, the only one known to exist, what I heard was simply stunning. The comments from that day in Council chambers had obviously been lost to time. But I was about to resurrect them.

But first, here's the backstory. I'll try to be brief.

Pennsylvania author Jane Jacobs' wrote in her 1961 book, *The Death and Life of Great American Cities*, "There is a widespread belief that Americans hate cities. I think it is probable that Americans hate city failure." And Harrisburg had plenty of failures.

Following the Second World War, few American cities were spared the next great generational movement. The returning GIs set out to create history's greatest living conditions—where life's most challenging decision includes which country club to join. The life they sought could no longer be found in urban dwellings. So they took their government loans, built families, and created the suburbs.

Similar to many historical migrations, it all started with the pursuit of a paycheck. As much as Harrisburg sought to modernize during the City Beautiful Movement, it was still an industrial city at heart. In its 200 years of production it manufactured engines, boilers, silk, cigars, typewriters and wheelbarrows. By the 1950s, those same plants supported more weeds than jobs. In part, with less to transport, the once invisible Pennsylvania Railroad— and others—were bankrupt.

These failures persuaded the city's remaining successes to flee. Billion dollar corporations like Rite Aid and Harsco, along with Central Penn College and the area's largest firms moved their corporate headquarters outside city limits. In the 1950s Harrisburgers drank their last hometown beer (Beers). Soon, the mall replaced the courthouse as the local meeting spot while Harrisburg passed Philly and Pittsburgh in per capita crime rates.

Those who invested most in the city during the early 20th century were passing on, and their heirs weren't interested in preserving what their parents had built. The new residents the capital city did attract had no connection to its history or future—and thus no stake in it.

Then, at the worst possible time, the government created two of the largest taxpayer funded programs in American history—highway and public school construction. For a population that professed small government politics, suburbanites more than anyone benefited from this form of centralized planning. Suddenly, you could live your entire life a mile from Harrisburg and never have to enter the city. And for many, that was reality.

Thus, Penn Harris Hotel went from 95 percent occupancy to 17 percent. What was once estimated to be 70 percent of the community's business became 11 percent for downtown Harrisburg (Beers). The city's first skyscraper was vacated. Other landmarks of the City Beautiful Movement were simply razed. We didn't just sacrifice great hunting lands and water purity—with suburbia we lost our history.

The explosion of television as an entertainment medium rendered city theaters unnecessary. One-by-one, Harrisburg's performing houses of art closed. The few that survived specialized in what the suburbs rejected: x-rated films. The Susquehanna River was no longer just a dividing line between Harrisburg and the west shore. It now separated the advantaged from the disadvantaged. The city lost its last vestige of political clout when its final resident Senator moved out in 1964 (Beers). It had officially been orphaned.

Mother Nature even seemed to hate Harrisburg. A Dutch Elm infestation in 1952 killed off the most beautiful aspect of the City Beautiful Movement: the tree lined canopy of Front Street.

After all that, the city desperately lacked money. To survive, it needed new revenue streams. That prompted the idea behind what may be the most monumental money suck in the history of American cities—The Resource Recovery Facility. Also known as the Harrisburg incinerator.

What was once the Pennsylvania Canal, was transformed into the stunning Wildwood Park during the City Beautiful Movement. By 1970, it had become a trash dump. A massive tire fire sparked debate concerning the park's new role. The construction of the incinerator was quickly approved—and it's been a lead weight on the city's budget ever since.

When it opened in the early 70s, what was supposed to cost $4.5 million, became $20 million. After it caught fire in 1978 and then partially collapsed a year later, $20 million became $30 (Beers). By 2000, the EPA threatened to close it down unless it modernized its pollution controls.

That brings us back to the City Council meeting on November 5, 2003. The city's elected leaders had a choice to make; do they guarantee a $125 million loan to update the ailing incinerator which had been shut down by the EPA, or do they cut ties forever with the facility?

As I listened to the recording of that night's meeting, most everyone was opposed to the project, except those that actually mattered.

"I'm telling you that this project will put the city into bankruptcy," proclaimed a wise Philadelphia resident from the group, Coalition Against the Incinerator. That resident spoke for 15 minutes to a packed room explaining how the numbers were wrong and why Council should not accept the loan.

"The city and the Authority don't have guaranteed waste streams," he passionately stated. "[These numbers are] over-estimating the potential power and steam sales, [and they] under estimate ash disposal and operating costs; and have no guarantee of an air pollution permit. This project will put the city into bankruptcy. But who will go first, residents or city hall?"

This is how then Mayor Stephen Reed's spokesman, Randy King, responded: "Everything that our opponents have said have been lies, distortions and untruths and things they have made up."

You can image my response when I first heard that. When I tried to get in touch with Mr. King to get comment on his comment, he didn't see a need to take my calls.

Either way, before Council's vote, dozens of residents spoke. One after another, they pled with Council not to approve the upgrade. And one after another, you just got the feeling Council didn't care. By the end of the night, only two residents supported the plan.

"And if you do this, the taxes are just going to keep going up and up and up," warned one resident.

"Please, think of seven generations down the road and don't do this," cried another.

Yet, despite overwhelming public rejection and the accurate warning of bankruptcy, Council voted 6-1 to accept the $125 million loan. This was a tearful, then, City Council member Linda Thompson justifying her "yes" vote.

"This has been no easy decision for me. With moral conviction I have prayed over this and I've prayed over this. And I've had intimate discussions with God. And my bible tells me let your yes be yes and let your no be no. And if 15 or 20 years from now it proves that I have made the wrong decision, charge it to my head and not my heart."

Mayor Thompson also wouldn't take my calls when I sought comment. Though, her fear of realizing a "wrong decision" 15 or 20 years later, turned out to be much sooner.

The audio of that Council meeting sent my mind racing. How could Council have been nearly unanimously wrong and the residents nearly unanimously right? It simply didn't add up. My natural inquisition is to find answers. But all my research only led me to more questions. Was I simply trying to bring reason to the unreasonable?

It wasn't until I was able to accept the true reach of Mayor Reed's influence that it all clicked. If Stephen Reed didn't endorse a candidate for Council, that candidate wouldn't win. Those six Council members weren't just voting for an incinerator project, they were securing their jobs.

From that point forward, as the city continued its collapse, I embarked on a personal mission. Law enforcement, at all levels, didn't appear interested in holding anyone accountable for murdering Harrisburg. So, I would.

Trust me. I know how pious that sounds. But I didn't get into TV news to be on TV. I don't do this job to make "special appearances," march in holiday parades or be a "celebrity judge." Please don't call me "talent" or a "TV personality." I'm a journalist who had before him an incredible journalistic opportunity.

Over the next few months, I filed a number of reports highlighting Reed failures, Mayor Thompson's incompetence and the facts behind the collapse. Some loved my work. Some hated it. But either way, I started making a name for myself. And that name earned me a phone call that's the dream of most every reporter.

I had just finished a chilly spring live shot on City Island. As I signed off, my phone turned on.

"Did this number come up blocked?" The voice on the other end was abrupt, yet slightly uncertain.

Intrigue quickly set in. "It did."

"Good! That was a hell of a story you did the other night." The man appeared nervous, yet comfortable. "My friends and I have been watching your reports for awhile, now." A dry cough accompanied his breaths. "You've done some nice work. Basically. No doubt about it."

"Well, thank you. I appreciate that." I didn't recognize his quirky tone. He appeared to be an older man, probably white, and fairly educated. I listened hard for language unique to a profession.

"How would you like the story of your career?" he asked with a slight chuckle.

I responded calmly, "Concerning what?"

"Listen, you're a young guy. You haven't been here long. Let me fill you in." His cough appeared systemic.

"Reed ran this town with an iron fist. He controlled everything, including the media, basically—no doubt about it."

"Yeah, I've heard that from a few people," I tried to sound less interested than I really was.

"A few people?" he gagged through his laugh. "It's a fact, basically—no doubt about it."

"Did you know him?"

"No," he snapped. "I wouldn't give that son-of-a-bitch the time of day."

His visceral reaction justified his call. This guy hated Reed and I had something he wanted.

"For years, my friends and I have been investigating that prick. He ruined this city. He needs to go to jail, basically—no doubt about it." Each time he coughed, it rang in my ear. He lacked the etiquette to separate the phone from his mouth. I felt that was telling.

"Listen," he gathered his breath. "Most people around this place love Reed. They think he's a god for how he saved the city. They don't want to know the truth. But there's some of us who do. Chris," he turned humble. "I think we can help each other."

"How's that?"

"We have some information for you. It won't be everything you need, but it could lead you in the right direction. I don't do computers. It'll be mailed."

"OK," I replied in earnest. "Can I get your name?"

"Maybe someday. We've worked with media in the past with success. If this works out, maybe we can do lunch."

"When can I expect the package?"

"In a couple days. Listen, there's a Federal grand jury in Williamsport that's investigating Reed. It's a big secret. I know you can't report that, now. But I'm telling you, it's true."

Suddenly, I became even more intrigued—if that were possible.

"This town has some incredible stories to tell if you're willing to dig for them." He paused with confidence. "And we think you're willing to put in the work. There's not many reporters that are, anymore." He then hung up.

With my heart and mind racing, I immediately dialed my station.

"Hey, did anyone call recently asking for my phone number?"

"I don't think so," answered my co-worker. "But, let me check."

A few seconds later I got the answer I expected, "Nope. Why? Were you expecting a call?"

"No," I replied honestly. "I wasn't. Just curious."

6: UNSPORTSMANLIKE

A FEW DAYS FOLLOWING that cryptic call, I received the package the man had promised. It came by way of a thick envelope with no return address. The station address was hand-penned in large block lettering and mailed from Harrisburg. The envelope appeared as secretive as the man himself.

I sat down at my desk with high expectations. And the man's bold predictions would not disappoint. The envelope, in its entirety, contained financial statements from a bank account opened in the early 90s. At immediate glance, the account was from a bank in Pottsville, about 55 miles northeast of the capital. The first action on the account was a deposit of $7 million. The next 10 pages detailed the massive withdrawals and smaller deposits. All the names were there: whom the money went to and how much. The proprietor of the account was Stephen Reed.

Line-by-line, I analyzed the document looking for names and companies I recognized. And there were plenty. Immediately, questions swirled throughout my head; where did this money come from? Was it all accounted for? How could Reed do this? Who was the man who sent me this? How did he get it?

I knew right away this story was months from air. First, I would have to corroborate every digit on every page. Then, set up the appropriate interviews and gather ancillary information. Of course, there was a good chance no one would be willing to talk on camera. I also knew I would have to confront Reed, himself. It had already been suggested by many that as a result of my reportage, I get a food taster. After this story, it was suggested I have someone start my car for me. But, I'm sure those comments were all in good fun.

From that point forward, the contents of that package became my obsession. I told few people and kept a low but proactive profile. I didn't need people talking. I needed people helping, which meant I needed few knowing.

This entire redirection of my career started with that one phone call. It gave me the confidence to pursue this level of investigative reporting. For that, I thank the nameless man. Yet it would be another call, one I'd receive soon after my series on Reed aired that would truly test my reporting ability. While combative and negative, that next call would eventually vindicate my pursuits and convince me to continue my work.

The only downside to receiving those bank statements lay in the timing. The city had just begun its steep decline towards history and I had to cover it. And as this process began its long, slow grind towards uncertainty, suffering city residents could only wait and hope the next crisis didn't affect them. But few, if any, would be spared.

Nearly every day I saw the pain and frustration the decisions of the prior few decades produced. And those who may have suffered most were part of the Harrisburg School District.

It isn't surprising that as the city fell apart so did its public education system. But what was surprising—at least to me—was the level of cuts proposed to deal with the problem. In 2011, the budget gap stood in the many millions. At first, the district, tried a slew of smaller cuts: some teachers, a couple aids, and a few programs. And for the most part, it kept the community at bay. But when the district announced its plans to eliminate kinder-garten, pre-k and all sports, the community erupted.

I had covered a number of Harrisburg School Board meetings over the previous year. Each time I found myself lamenting how few parents were involved. Harrisburg's a district of about 6,500 students. But just a few dozen parents would show up every other Monday—and it was always the same ones.

The meetings were held on the first floor of a small office building far from any campus. The normally half empty room sat 65 uncomfortably. Its white laminate floors and tiled ceiling seemed more appropriate for interrogations than educational discussions. Most subur-ban board meetings were held in the school auditorium, where the members sit perched atop a stage shadowed by theater lighting. During Harrisburg's meetings, everyone sat on the same level and was lit with the same un-flattering florescent light.

When I was assigned to cover the board meeting following the announcements of the cuts, I was told by the assignment desk to arrive early. My station expected a large turnout.

"Have you ever been to a Harrisburg school board meeting?" I asked condescendingly. "No one shows up."

This is one of those times I was happy to be wrong. On this night, the room was made uncomfortable not by boredom, but by humid air and hot tempers. The attendees spilled out so deep into the hallway, most could only hear what was happening. Those stuffed inside were outraged and rightfully so.

My photographer and I didn't make any friends as we forced our way through the crowd. We ended up crammed toward the back near a speaker. The room that previously sat 65 somehow fit a few hundred—and no one was willing to relinquish their space.

One-by-one frustrated and irritated parents stomped to the podium and lashed out at the school board.

"How can you sleep at night knowing what you're doing to our kids," one parent yelled, jabbing her elongated fingernails at the superintendent.

Another parent added, "What do you think is going to happen to this city when all those kids in sports don't have sports, no more? All of them will be on the streets from the time school is out until they go to bed. Do the math." The panic in her voice was real.

A calmer professional looking lady opined, "I'm a working mother. I have a hard time paying for daycare during the summer. Now, you want to take pre-k and kindergarten away. How am I supposed to survive?" Her voice cracked with disappointment.

Each parent who addressed the board made their point and made it well. And the rowdy crowd was not shy in showing its approval. Few speakers made it through their statement without being interrupted with applause, yells, or cheers. With a raw and potent energy, the residents had come alive.

"These changes will be disruptive to the educational environment. We know that," admitted one school official. She spoke in-between parents. I think her intent was to calm the crowd with reason and understanding. It didn't work. "We just don't have the resources to do all these things that other districts can do."

She explained how the district failed to properly apply for $7 million in grants that it had budgeted for the previous year. The district had recently descended into chaos when Mayor Thompson inexplicably fired its white superintendent and hired the black one. Without his leadership, that $7 million in grants was lost in the transition. "These are painful, terribly, terribly painful sacrifices that the administration is asking the community to buy into," continued the same official.

"We're losing everything," cried one parent from the back. "We're losing our community."

A very large black woman in very bright colors stood up and pumped her fist. "How in 2012 can any child not have kindergarten? It makes me sick!"

As the room exploded in approval, I glanced over at the black gentleman who had been standing next to me the entire meeting. He had deep wrinkles, thick glasses and thin gray hair. I didn't get the impression he had a child in the school. He was just concerned.

"This ain't right," he said to me, his voice calm but serious.

I nodded my head. And I did genuinely agree with him.

"I bet this would never happen where you're from." His polite tone lacked any semblance of animus or malice. He just stated a fact, and then turned to further observe the up-heaving room.

Had he yelled that statement at me, said it in disgust or added a few expletives, I probably would have accepted it better. But the basic understanding in his delivery hit hard because he was right. This would never have happened in my high school. And indeed, it was not fair—especially since the fault was not that of the young victims.

I was too young to understand any advantage kindergarten afforded me. And I certainly can't speak to what I learned in Pre-K. But I can say unequivocally that organized sports played a huge role in shaping the adult I would become. To this day, I can directly relate athletic lessons to successes in my professional and personal life. To think every kid in Harrisburg would lose out on that was heartbreaking. And to think those most responsible were never held accountable was infuriating.

But it didn't always used to be this way. In fact, it used to be the exact opposite. Not a century earlier, Harrisburg had some of the best schools in the nation. In 1919, the district had 15,000 students, nearly three times its 2012 enrollment. Many of these students lived outside the city and paid tuition (Beers). Now, any tuition from Harrisburg is sent to the suburbs.

With a proud emphasis on education, the city regularly graduated Ivy League students. And with the strong academics came powerful athletics. Throughout the early 20th Century during the City Beautiful Movement, Harrisburg fielded a number of state champion football teams. The Central High Capitolians won eight Keystone State titles. Harrisburg Tech won four, plus a national title in 1919. In that year the team went 12-0 and never gave up a point. Today, neither school exists.

But as went the city, so went the city schools. As wealth moved away, poverty settled in. And it happened quickly. Harrisburg schools were 12 percent black in 1930. Fifty years later, they were 80 percent minority. By the late 70s, the district had a 30 percent withdrawal rate. Although, it should be pointed out, that was a number the administrators considered misleading since 24 of their students during those years actually went to jail and didn't technically withdrawal (Beers).

Some have argued the Harrisburg School District's greatest achievement in the 70s was simply staying open. In addition to all its other problems that decade, city athletics were banned from playing suburban schools. During a fight at a football game, six fans were injured and went to the hospital. Everyone arrested for the brawl was black. Four of the seven minorities were indicted. Three went to prison. To punish the city, suburban schools formed their own athletic conference leaving Harrisburg students with nowhere to play. They were forced to drive hours to find opponents (Beers).

For the next 20 years, the district floundered. But in 2000, it got some new leadership. With the school failing badly, the state appointed Mayor Stephen Reed to fix it. He became the first mayor to take on this role in Pennsylvania's history. Soon after, he imposed a massive reform and rehabilitation project—sound familiar?

Reed's successes with the city were only rivaled by his achievements as school district administrator. His educational performance was a big reason he was named the third best mayor in the world in 2006 by World Mayor. It was said of the Mayor:

"Mr. Reed's performance as Mayor, and his well-earned reputation as someone uniquely suited to transforming problems into triumphs, prompted the Pennsylvania Legislature to give him control over the Harrisburg City School District. Since that time, the district's performance measures have steadily improved. In the last five years, graduation rates are up 71 per cent, students continuing to higher education are up 263 per cent. Mr. Reed also took on the challenge of starting up, from scratch, a 4-year city-based university, the Harrisburg University of Science & Technology. This is just one of many examples of an idea that was at first scoffed at by many in the local and regional communities, only to be later applauded." (It's also worth pointing out that—as of this book's publication—the future of Harrisburg University is uncertain. It's having a hard time paying its bills.)

When Mayor Reed's candidacy for World Mayor was announced, the city rallied behind him in all his achievements.

"I am a 11th grade student, at Harrisburg High School. Thanks, Mayor Reed for giving me all of the opportunities I have. I have a safer walk home now, thanks to you."

"Mayor Reed has devoted his many terms in office to make Harrisburg what it is today. He has turned the Harrisburg School District around 100%. Scores are on the rise, graduation rates have increased dramatically and people are no longer afraid to dine in one of the many nice restaurants along 2nd Street or visit the city for its festivities throughout the summer months. He is a Mayor who lives, eats, sleeps and breathes the city he was hired to serve. He deserves the World Mayor Award."

"Since he gained control of the city school system several years ago, the school system has made incredible strides in rebounding from decades of decline. Mayor Reed deserves recognition for his dedication to the city of Harrisburg and the city owes him a debt of gratitude. Many comment that he is 'Mayor for Life' or as long as he wants the title. I cannot imagine any individual more deserving of the World Mayor title than Stephen R. Reed, who is truly a Mayor extraordinaire."

"Stephen Reed has committed his very soul to public service and is a tireless and positive force for change and improvement. Over the years, he has taken our tired, grey city and filled it with life and color and he always gives the impression that he has only just begun. He is a leader and wastes no time in party politics."

"Mayor Stephen Reed has dedicated his life to improving the City of Harrisburg. Even tonight as I nominate him for World Mayor, he is watching the river and activating plans to [ensure] citizens are safe if the rain continues to fall and the river floods."

"Mayor Reed has made many changes in the Harrisburg area, and Harrisburg school district. While growing up in Hershey Pennsylvania, Harrisburg was not a place that I was allowed to visit. Now that I'm 41, I work downtown, and allow my teenage sons to come here."

"We're proud of Harrisburg and its re-creator, our very own 'Superman', Steve Reed!"

"Harrisburg's Mayor has turned our city from an impov-erished and seedy dump to a lively, fun, and beautiful place to live. Stevie should definitely win."

"Stephen Reed is Mr. Harrisburg. Since becoming mayor in 1982, he has led a revival and growth for Pennsylvania's capital city, which was unthinkable when he assumed office. Harrisburg has won numerous awards since Mayor Reed began his term of office including Tree City USA, All American City, Forbes Magazine list of places where Employees' Dollars Goes Further, and awards for Police Accreditation."

"Steve Reed is absolutely the most dynamic, committed, brilliant visionary who gets things done. We could not pay him enough to do the job he does for love of the citizens of Harrisburg. Steve Reed Mayor of the World for LIFE."

"He is virtually Mayor for life of Harrisburg. Mayor of the world is the next logical step."

"The Mayor has created an environment in which urban youth can triumph. Mayor Reed is the hope for America, not just the City of Harrisburg!"

Unfortunately, much like the city, soon after Reed relinquished control of the school district, it too collapsed. Somehow, graduation rates went from 79 percent in 2010 to 38 percent just two years later.

In case you're wondering, the Harrisburg School District still has kindergarten and sports. The city ended up "finding" $11 million in the budget it didn't know it had.

7: UNSPORTSMANLIKE II

WHILE HARRISBURG PUBLIC SCHOOLS fiddled with eliminating the entire sports program, Mayor Thompson was certainly getting her game on.

The capital city is not foreign to great athletes. Christy Mathewson, a member of Major League baseball's inaugural Hall of Fame class, played in Harrisburg. So did Hall of Famer Eddie Plank. Jim Thorpe played ball for the Harrisburg Indians, a minor league squad, and honed his craft via other city sports. As did 1925 NFL champion running back Carl Beck. That year, his Pottsville Maroons beat the Green Bay Packers 31-0 and the Chicago Cardinals (now in Arizona) 21-7 to win the national title. Babe Ruth and Willie Mays also made stops in Harrisburg during their professional careers—both hit home runs some argue have yet to land. Even "The Clown Prince of Baseball," Max Patkins, called Harrisburg home. And Hall of Fame announcer, Andy Musser, was once a Harrisburg Senators batboy (Beers).

But of all the athletes and athletic feats witnessed by capital city spectators, it could be argued nothing quite compares to the basketball skills once displayed by Mayor

Linda Thompson. Although, the fascination with her athleticism was not due to her athleticism.

2011 was yet another violent year in the city. It's sad to say, but crime had become so customary that victims simply existed in newsrooms as numbers. The first murder of the year still garnered some attention, but by October the press grew bored. With gangs, drugs and disadvantaged families, most crime seemed to exist in a vacuum—where nearly identical stories were only made different by the names of those involved. Eventually crime was so common it was less newsworthy. Violent felonies had become expected and therefore less interesting.

But then, the city was rocked by the murder of a young man named Thorin Burgess, who wasn't like other victims. Burgess was a 19-year-old recent graduate of John Harris High School in Harrisburg. He had a job and no criminal record. He was a kid who just loved to play basketball, and his home court was Reservoir Park.

Reservoir Park is yet another aspect of the City Beautiful Movement. It's 85 acres of calming grass, hills and trees. On a warm June night, Burgess was playing a game of pick-up in one of the many enclosed courts. It's not an uncommon spot for hundreds of people to gather and cheer. As this particular day faded, the court settled under the shadow of the Civil War Museum, which looms atop the hill. Above the rims, the lights began to flicker. Below the rims, the peace would soon be lost.

Shortly before 8:00, an argument broke out between Burgess' 17-year-old brother and 19-year-old Darnell Williams. When the tension escalated, Burgess ran over to break it up. Out of nowhere, Williams brandished a gun. A wrestling match ensued. People on the court scattered while those outside the fence ran for cover. Then, a single gunshot sent a bullet into Burgess' liver. Before settling in his right lung, it ripped through his torso.

The young man with a seemingly bright future collapsed onto the court. As his life slowly drained onto the warm concrete, Williams ran away. An ambulance was called, but it wouldn't matter. The young man would quickly bleed out.

"I feel like it's my fault," Burgess' distraught brother would later tell the media. "I feel like I could have stopped it. I could have prevented it, and I didn't."

By the time I arrived on scene following the shooting, Burgess' body had been removed. Police had already done their interviews and took their pictures. The court was empty for the exemption of one crying teenager and a teddy bear.

"I hate Harrisburg," the boy said as I approached him. His lungs pulsed as he tried to speak. Though it was June, his grey hoodie was pulled tight over his head. I could barely see his face. "I don't understand. Why do people do this?" He tried to swipe away the tears as quickly as they fell, but he couldn't keep up.

"I'm sorry," I replied in a near whisper. "Did you know Thorin well?"

The boy, who looked to be about 16, kept his stare towards the ground. "I don't want to talk," he sobbed. "Please leave."

I turned to my photographer and nodded. I wasn't going to press the young man. He had clearly been through a lot.

As I walked around the outside of the court, I saw a street so depressed few homes appeared livable. You could tell these were once gorgeous properties. Most were three full stories with moulded porches and bay windows. Now, some were missing roofs and few had doors. I saw plenty of plywood, but little glass.

"Those homes were really something 35 years ago." A reporter from a rival station approached me. He had been in the market since his discharge from Vietnam. If anyone would know, it'd be him. "These homes were the managers of the factories and mills. The laborers and workers lived in the row homes a few blocks that way. The owners had those mansions on Front Street."

"It breaks my heart to see beautiful homes rot," I told him. "It's such a waste."

"Look at the wood work. Look at the architecture." He gestured forward with a wrinkled hand. "That stuff is expensive to repair. People around here can't afford that. These will all be torn down eventually. Or, they'll fall down. One of the two."

Following a few un-awkward seconds of reflective silence, I heard, "Chris!" I turned to see my photographer waving.

"Excuse me, Jim." He nodded as I walked away.

"What do you have?" I approached my photog slowly. I was not too energized.

He pointed down to the spot where the young man's blood had congealed. Police cleaned most of it, but they failed to get it all.

"What do you want to do with it?" he asked me. The loose fence surrounding us began to rattle in the steady wind. Some dark clouds had formed in the west. For June, the wind had a mild bite.

"Shoot it," I replied in full sigh. "We'll decide later if we'll use it."

With him focusing his shot, I wandered the court in search of anything newsworthy. I'm not sure how I didn't notice sooner, but off to the side someone had begun a memorial. In the coming days, it would grow into a giant remembrance. But at this point, it was only two small glass candles flanking a teddy bear.

The bear was red and white, with a big red nose and joyful smile. It didn't look new. But it didn't look used, either. The foot high toy rested gently against the chain link fence. Its feet comfortably hung over the concrete curb that surrounded the court. He looked happy and innocent—as if he were watching his favorite team win. On his belly, in bold lettering, someone wrote, "RIP T-Boy. We Love You. You Will Be Missed."

Immediately following this highly visible murder, the community demanded action from city leadership. The only problem was action takes money. And the city didn't have any. Not only that, but the proposed financial recovery plan, yet to be approved, called for 19 city positions to be eliminated, which included park rangers. Another 43 public safety positions, including the Street Crimes Unit, Traffic Safety Unit and walking patrols, would be cut later if needed.

The night of Burgess' murder, Harrisburg only had three park rangers on payroll and they didn't carry weapons. Nevertheless, none were around when he was killed.

Mayor Linda Thompson quickly responded to the murder, and public demands, by calling for more police foot and bike patrols. She was never quite clear on how these officers would be paid, or from what assignments they would be pulled. She just kept saying, "Public safety is our number one concern."

When Burgess' autopsy was announced, the county coroner Graham Hetrick, who's a character unique to himself (such that he was the focus of a pilot filmed in late 2013 for a reality show for the A&E network called "Graham of Evidence"), denounced Thompson's plan to combat crime by saying it would do little. He argued police can't be everywhere. And you won't change the murder rate until you change societal values.

Possibly disturbed by the reaction to her reaction, Mayor Thompson called for a press conference. It was held on the basketball court at the site of the murder. With the memorial in the background, Thompson spoke in a stern tone. She was surrounded by police officers: some in traditional uniform and some on bikes with bright orange vests.

The media formed a semi-circle a few yards in front of Thompson's podium. Off to the side, members of the community slowly trickled in. There was little noise and no smiles. The stains of Burgess' blood had yet to fade from the court's surface.

"[Williams] needs to turn himself in immediately, or otherwise he will remain a hunted criminal," Mayor Thompson stated with authority. She told the media she spoke to William's family and asked them to encourage the suspect to surrender. She then said something about someone in Williams' family having a connection with God and possibly a local pastor and how that could mean God will convince Williams to do the right thing. I don't know. That's the best way I can describe it.

Either way, she answered a slew of important questions about public safety, the responsibility of park rangers and the community. It was a serious press conference with serious questions and serious concerns. It had the ability to formulate strong headlines and send a powerful message. But at the end, true to form, Thompson stole the lead.

With the media packing up, the 50-year-old Mayor walked over to a young neighborhood boy in a red shirt. He was sitting quietly off to the side and didn't seem desirous of attention.

"Let me see that basketball," she demanded. The boy was hesitant to give it up.

"Come on," she repeated harshly. "Let me see it."

The boy clearly was not interested in playing games.

But when the Mayor snatched the ball from the boy's hands, every photographer snatched their cameras off their tripods. As their toggle lights flicked on, the Mayor ostensibly began dribbling the ball atop the victim's bloodstains. A more astonishing sight, I cannot recall.

In four-inch black pumps and a pin stripped suit, she then drove hard to the hoop, proclaiming, "I know how to play ball. I used to play ball in my younger years... people get jealous."

She took a quick shot that bricked off the rim. Gathering her rebound, she shot again. "Woohoo!!" She yelled and clapped as the ball went into the hoop. With the mayor celebrating, the boy rushed to get his ball.

As he walked away thinking it was over, the Mayor called him out. "Hey, how about a game of one-on-one?"

He largely ignored her and continued walking with his head down. We can only assume this young man knew the murder victim—as many of the attendees did.

"Come on," the Mayor continued. "Man up!" Yes, she actually said that.

Upon hearing her insult, the boy regretfully turned. Out of courtesy, and with sunken shoulders, he gently tossed her the ball. Thompson then fired it back at him. The young teenager instinctively reacted.

"Don't ease up because she's the Mayor," the chief of police called out. Reluctantly, he checked the ball.

Before the boy knew it, the Mayor jammed her ass into his stomach, bouncing him backwards. She leaned back onto her heels and dribbled hard with both hands. In short bursts, she forced her way towards the basket. The boy offered very light resistance. The Mayor then faked right, turned left and launched a shot. She missed.

"I almost had it in," she called out. "Come on!"

The boy again tried to get away. But she grabbed the ball and fired a sneak shot from the foul line. Air ball.

"Too short," she proclaimed.

Likely fearing the consequences, the boy chased the ball and threw it back to her.

"Don't be laughin'," she commanded as he tossed it. "This is one-on-one."

She took another shot from the foul line. Missed again.

"Ohh, almost had it," she laughed uncomfortably.

He retrieved it.

She shot again. The ball ricocheted hard off the backboard.

"It's all in the wrist," she affirmed. The media cameras were glued.

After two more missed shots, the Mayor flicked her hair and strutted to the podium. "I have to get back to work, now."

Meanwhile, the boy was left to chase his ball, which had bounced towards the memorial.

The media was speechless—along with nearly everyone else.

I think it was at that moment, the media realized we must follow this woman everywhere she goes—and a camera must always be on.

Williams was eventually caught, convicted and sentenced to 22-44 years for the murder. We never did air the shots of the young man's blood on the court—out of respect for the family.

8: A ROTTING BEAUTY

"HOW'S THE STORY COMING?"

The man's voice had quickly grown less uncertain and more confident. It had now been a few months since we first spoke. And every few weeks I had grown accustomed to receiving calls from his blocked number.

"I think it's coming along well," I replied. Even though we had developed a good relationship, there was no need for pleasantries. I still didn't even know the guy's name. Plus, he wasn't calling to chat.

"Do you think you have a good story?" He forced a hard cough directly into my ear. I never had the heart to tell him how much I loathed his tact. I guess a part of me was afraid to learn the cause behind the hack.

"I think we have a *great* story," I said honestly. "I just need some people to come forward."

"I can't do that!" he snapped. "We can't go on the record."

My statement was not intended for him. "But if you can find someone, that would be helpful."

"We can keep giving you information and point you in the right direction. But that's it, basically—no doubt about it."

"I understand," I raised my voice slightly. "But, you may have noticed the city's taking a giant shit right now. It's consuming all my time. But I'm positive. I will get this stuff on air. People need to see this. People need to know this."

"Just make sure you let me know when it airs," he demanded. "I have a lot of people who want to see it. You're developing a good reputation, basically—no doubt about it. People are talking. A lot of people are talking."

"I'll let you know when I know."

"Good. I'll tell the guys."

"Please do."

"Listen, here's another tip for you. Go to the prothonotary. You can see who has donated to Reed's campaigns over the years and compare that to the names in that bank account we gave you. You will notice many of those names are the same. That's how Reed worked. If you didn't give him money, you didn't get contracts in the city, basically—no doubt about it." He gagged over those last few syllables. "He held complete control. Everything that happened in Harrisburg happened through him."

"I think my reports will make that clear," I replied.

"How's the wife?"

I was pretty sure I never told him I was married, but I played along. "She's fine."

"Any kids in the future?"

"Possibly."

"Have you told her that we're working together?"

"I mentioned something about it."

"Good." He coughed once. "Glad to hear it." He coughed twice. "We'll be in touch." With a click, he was gone.

As much as I wanted to tell the man more, I didn't. The fact was, the bank information he gave me led me to even better stories. Because so many people in the city were beholden to Reed, or feared his retribution, most wouldn't dare speak ill of him. But during his seven terms in office, he made plenty of enemies. My task was to find them and convince them to talk. Fortunately, the greatest motivation for getting people to talk is anger and frustration—something of which Harrisburg had plenty.

Once I found those people, I began to learn the real story. Some invited me to their homes. Others preferred to meet in parks or restaurants. One person would simply pull me into a corner of the atrium after City Council meetings. I always find it interesting how some want to talk to known journalists out in the open while others preferred to chat in secret. I personally couldn't care less, either way.

But, no matter the tactic, the story was coming together. Question after question after question, I was beginning to understand the real Stephen Reed. Beyond the media glorification and the community adoration, the hidden pieces of his true actions were being uncovered.

It seemed the more information I acquired, the more people were willing to talk. Perhaps they felt more comfortable knowing my interest was real. They had been let down by the media for decades, trust was a struggle.

"Finally, someone is willing to look into this stuff," people would tell me. Of everything I heard, those statements were probably the most difficult to accept—in full deference to my colleagues in the Harrisburg press.

It was during this time, in between receiving the bank statement and the first story airing, that I learned of "The Reed Team" and "The Reed Machine." The "Mayor for Life" was able to consolidate his power in a way that these two terms—which should have been warning signs to the community—became jovial clichés, nuanced wisecracks or even terms of endearment. When my stories would air, they would simply be referenced for what they were: the modus operandi of a despot.

It was also during this time—in between receiving the bank statement and the first story airing—that I first met, LeTarsha Richardson. The city had recently been plagued with sinkholes and she was the latest victim. The infrastructure laid during the City Beautiful Movement, and prior, was now more than a century old, and in dire need of repairs.

Dozens of sinkholes had opened in the year prior. The biggest just happen to drop directly in front of Richardson's home. It was New Year's Eve and the city had found itself gripped in a bitter cold snap. The sewage and water pipes that ran in front of her home were more than 125 years old. Decades ago, they sprung tiny leaks. Over time, those tiny leaks eroded large gaps under the road. These holes can be detected—and addressed—before they create havoc, but that takes effort, money and leadership— commodities the city lacked.

When this hole on North Fourth Street opened, it encompassed the entire road. When I arrived shortly after it fell, I had never seen anything like it. It was the day after New Year's. I was greatly enjoying an early dinner with my family in suburban Philadelphia when I got the call. We were all together: my mom, dad, wife, brother, sister-in-law and nephew.

"Hey, we need you to come in." As much as newsroom assignment desk managers try to act caring and understanding, they usually fail miserably. There is no call a reporter or photog dreads more than the early call on a holiday—especially when the news can wait. I once had a photographer program his phone so when the desk rang, his caller ID would read, "Hell."

"I'm eating with my family," I replied, most likely with a mouthful of meat and starch. "Can it wait an hour or two?"

"A massive sinkhole opened on Fourth Street," he informed me. "The entire street is shut down. All the homes are being evacuated. The utilities have been shut off. It's cold as shit. People are pissed. The Mayor is missing. We need you here."

"Son-of-a-bitch," I moaned. "The sinkhole's not going anywhere. Can't we have one day without chaos?"

"Apparently not," he replied. "See you soon. Dress warmly."

I looked over at my wife. I could tell a mild to medium annoyance had set in. "You'll get overtime for this, right?" She asked.

I could not have been less enthusiastic as I finished my plate, "yeah."

Minutes later, I was scraping the ice off my windshield in preparation for a 61 mile drive west.

At the time, our station live trucks were not much younger than I was. If it didn't have 300,000 miles, it wasn't worth mentioning.

"Let's hope we get some heat from this old girl today." My photographer had just finished loading his gear when I entered the garage.

"Why the hell did we have to come in early?" I said in disgust as I settled down inside. "The damn hole will still be there in two hours."

With a turn of the key, the engine squeaked and lurched to life. "Why do you ask these questions?" He looked over at me in a calm disbelief. "Haven't you learned?"

The sinkhole was only a few blocks from the station. The truck wasn't even close to warm by the time we arrived. When the wheels came to a stop, I secured my leather gloves, wool hat and black scarf. With a kick of the door, I stepped out into the winter.

As expected, the neighborhood was barren and quiet. No kids, no lights, no anything. The street was closed nearly two blocks in both directions from the hole. I waited for my photog to grab his gear before walking.

"Want me to carry that?" I asked of the tripod.

"Not at all," he replied as he hoisted the sticks onto his shoulder. "The extra work keeps me warmer. I'll save your offer for July."

I smiled as he slammed and locked the door.

The walk to the hole was brutal. Within seconds my ears began to burn while my hands sought warmth deep within the pockets of my wool trench coat. Why when it's freezing, does the wind always seem to blow in your face?

Based on what the desk described, I was expecting a big hole. What it ended up being was far more impressive. It spanned the entire width of the road: perhaps 30 feet long and just as deep. The ground was so eroded the only remnants inside were large chunks of painted asphalt.

"Wow," my photog exclaimed as he set up his sticks. "How does this happen?"

"I know," I replied equally perplexed. "It doesn't seem possible."

The hole was so deep you could see the varying layers of dirt, rock and city development. The old leaky pipes that caused the problem could only be seen peeking out the sides. Had it not been a heavily overcast day, I'm sure the icicles growing below the copper tubes would have stunningly reflected the sun.

The utilities on the street had already been disconnected. Twenty-nine partially dilapidated town homes had already been evacuated. A dozen or so other fully dilapidated homes were abandoned. Most of the residents went to friends' or families' homes. Some went to shelters. But in the back of one home I did notice a single reddish light. At first I thought it was a candle someone had left burning. But the more I watched, the less it flickered.

"Hey," I whacked my photog on the arm and pointed.

"I thought no one could stay here," he remarked. "Why would you want to?"

Seconds later, we were knocking on a splintered door. When it opened, I felt no heat rushing out.

A large, middle-aged black woman draped in multiple layers of sweats appeared before me, "Can I help you?" The half-moons under her eyes were the deepest black I had ever seen.

"My name's Chris Papst from CBS 21."

"Yeah, I know," she interrupted. "What do you want?" I looked down and saw a little covered head pop out from behind her leg. Another, about the same age, emerged from the other side. The tips of my fingers had grown numb inside my gloves.

"We're here covering the sinkhole and saw that you have a light on."

"It's my space heater," she again interrupted—making no attempt to hide her resentment.

"Ummm," I stuttered. "Would you mind if we ask you some questions for the news tonight about what you're dealing with? It might help get the city's attention."

"Do it, mom." The high voice of a third little person walked up behind her. Her face was thoroughly covered. I could only see dark brown dots floating in big white circles.

"How many kids do you have?" I asked with a chuckle. "They just keep coming."

Her mouth curled up, "I got seven wonderful babies."

I'm not quite sure what my physical reaction was, but that was not the answer I expected.

"Go right ahead and ask some questions," she said pulling a fourth child from behind her. "I ain't got nothing else to do but complain."

"Do you want your kids in the shot?" which I usually asked out of courtesy.

"Of course," she stated with certainty as she arranged her brood in front of her. "Get them all in the shot. They deserve some airtime."

I couldn't help but smile at her blunt approach.

With her kids lined up like wrapped dolls, I interviewed the family with their front door wide open.

"This has been bad. This is horrible," she told me. "I've never been through nothing like this before." LeTarsha was very honest and didn't hold back. Most of her kids were school-aged. She had no husband. No job. No heat. No shower.

When she spoke to me, only one sinkhole had opened —with its edge not far from her stoop. In the coming days, a second would accompany it; then a third. The entire block lost water, gas and sewer services. As the river began to freeze, so did the water in her toilets. She and her children spent the day bundled and cuddled around a portable space heater—waiting.

The Red Cross—not the city—offered the family shelter, but she wasn't interested. "I'm not going to no shelter," she snapped. "I'm not taking my kids to a shelter with people I don't know." But their options for suitable shelter were limited. Her children couldn't even warm up at school—this was how they spent their winter break.

"We got a Mayor (Linda Thompson) and everything, that's not doing nothing to help this neighborhood. Because I feel this was not our fault. We shouldn't have to supply everything [like maintained utilities] for ourselves." The family's misery lasted nearly a week when the utilities finally returned. But, the road would be closed for months as the city sought funds for a proper repair.

Harrisburg has miles of old pipes, making sinkholes a popular sight. The ones outside LeTarsha's house first appeared as small ones a year-and-a-half earlier. But they were not addressed and expanded. In reality, it's probably more accurate to say they were ignored. This was a poor neighborhood populated mostly by renters. No one seemed to care.

As I finished interviewing LeTarsha, the city's Communications Director walked up to the sinkhole to take a look. So, I walked up to him to talk.

"How do you stop something like this from happening?" he said. "You don't. It's very difficult." At 5'8" with gray hair and little personality, he was the city's most skilled propagandist.

He went on to tell me the Department of Public Works was inspecting Harrisburg's 150 miles of pipeline looking for leaks and erosion that could cause more sinkholes. He said it's a huge endeavor, which I asked why the Mayor hadn't started the process long ago.

"We didn't know the extent of the problem," he explained in a near frozen state. "The previous administration left us no information on the condition of the underground pipes." He might be right, but I was tired of politicians blaming problems on their predecessors. College coaches, professional coaches, and CEOs of major corporations never blame their issues on what they inherited. Why do we allow our elected leaders that luxury?

"The future is arriving all across the Commonwealth, not only here but all cities with aging infrastructure." I guess he felt the need to explain that Harrisburg is not alone and therefore his boss, Mayor Thompson, was not at fault. "Something has to be done at the federal and state level to help take care of this situation."

"Come on, Bob," I lamented. "People are suffering. Go talk to the family in that house. Have Mayor Thompson talk to them. Something needs to be done on a local level, now. This isn't right. This is not these people's fault."

He didn't disagree. But he also didn't seem interested in defending the administration.

"That woman is upset," I continued pointing at her front door. "And she should be. She just wants something to be done. She wants someone to care about her and her family. That's the mayor's job."

"I assure you, Chris," he replied. "The Mayor is working hard."

It took every nugget of professionalism I had to not laugh in his face. The taxpayers of Harrisburg paid him a lot of money to tell me that. Meanwhile, nothing was being done and the people were mired in anguish.

Despite Bob's roll as the Mayor's chief propagandist—something I detested—we did get along. I just had to keep reminding myself he was the Mayor's spokesman, not the people's. Either way, he was a nice guy who found himself in a nearly impossible situation. In reality, if it weren't for him, Mayor Thompson probably wouldn't have finished her term. Bob's glib rhetoric and calm disposition placated the mob.

After we finished talking business—as usual—we hit on less pressing topics. While in discussion, I notice what looked to be small railroad tracks a few feet below the road. They too had collapsed into the hole. But the ends were still visible.

"What is that?" I asked him.

He smiled as much as he could given his mouth was likely as numb as mine. "Those are the old trolley tracks. A hundred years ago, trolleys ran all over the city. It's from a time when the city didn't have these types of problems." He chuckled. "In fact, many of the problems we have are because of what was built a hundred years ago when Harrisburg had loads of money. Now, much of it needs maintained and we can't afford it."

"It would have been neat if some of those tracks were usable," I commented. "A trolley would be a neat feature in the city."

He nodded, slowly.

Underground infrastructure improvements are an expenditure that can't be seen and therefore can't be used for political expedience. Ergo, it's not uncommon for water and sewage pipes not to be addressed until necessary—and necessity oftentimes lies in crises. So, Mayor Thomp-son's degree of fault is questionable. But much like the financial crisis—something else entirely not her fault—she did receive plenty of criticism for not having an emergency plan ready.

With homeowners and tenants being evacuated following the sinkhole on North Fourth, their homes were open targets for criminals—and many were looted. During subsequent City Council meetings, the Mayor was blasted for not anticipating that by increasing police patrols in that area. Of course, the Mayor's abhorrence of City Council meant she wasn't at the meetings to hear these complaints, but I'm sure she was watching on the city's public access channel—which despite the financial crisis somehow maintained a budget.

Making matters worse, most all the sinkholes sunk in low-income, depressed areas—an uncomfortable fact that didn't help heal a city geographically divided by racial and class lines.

By 2013, lacking money and leadership, Harrisburg had found itself in a state of perpetual rot—for the second time in 40 years. The first rot happened in the 1970s when city life had become taboo. During this decade, America did not simply favor suburbs; it ostensibly despised cities. Not until the second decade of the 21st century was the value of urban living again realized. But during that 40-year period, Harrisburg and other cities were largely seen as nebulous holes where tax dollars went to die. Beyond sending their money there, suburbanites had little interest in going there, themselves.

The depressing part of that reality is what was lost when cities failed. America joyfully sacrificed decades if not centuries of history that we will never get back. There was once a small photography shop in Harrisburg said to be the oldest in the nation. Its technology was used in capturing the terrifying images of carnage at Gettysburg. Now it's gone along with many other businesses and structures that either collapsed, were razed or are too far rotted to be saved.

As the baby boomers abandoned urban living, land values tanked encouraging non-profits to fill the void. This ensured Harrisburg and other cities a suffocated tax base. To this day, more than 50 percent of the capital city's real estate is made up of state-owned buildings, churches, schools and other non-profits that don't pay taxes. Add to that a third of the population that lives in poverty. How can it possibly prosper?

That desperate need for revenue has spawned a near endless fight over PILOT (Payment In Lieu of Taxes) payments, which has further soured local relationships. Cities argue that non-profits need to pay their fair share. Non-profits point to the workers they employ, the parking spots they buy or lease, and the city establishments they frequent, as enough.

It's a logical argument. However, if it were truly enough, why was the city forced to build a school without interior walls in the 1970s? And why in that same decade, did a local newspaper reporter refer to the city's downtown as, "depressed and bombed-out?"

The fact is people hated cities. And perhaps they should have. Even to the most casual of observers, Harrisburg couldn't do anything but waste tax dollars. The capital once tried to garner publicity by breaking the Guinness World Record for participants in a tug of war. Instead of receiving positive headlines and injecting the city with much needed pride, it was laughed at when 200 students got rope burn and 80 went to the hospital. Five teenagers lost fingers or fingertips when the rope snapped.

From the outside looking in, the most thriving industry in Harrisburg may have been retail prostitution. In 1972 alone, 129 ladies of the night were arrested along with 214 of their clients (Beers). Some used the fact that no mayor of Harrisburg had ever been elected to higher office, as a way to prove the office's inferiority. That may have also been substantiated when the city's two main hospitals discontinued their ambulance service, creating a grave public safety hazard. During that decade of rot, Harrisburg had no convention centers, stadiums, libraries or tourist bureaus to attract people (Beers). In a matter of 50 years, Harrisburg went from looking down on the suburbs to being looked down upon by them. It was so bad in the 70s that the city considered selling city hall, a middle school, the water system and its sculptures (Beers).

Of course, corruption was also an ingredient in this fecal cocktail. In the 70s, the Chief of Police was charged and found guilty of larceny and two of his officers were convicted of not paying the IRS its rightful share. A state audit showed the city lost 20,000 traffic tickets, but it discovered fraudulent lumbering in city woods. Meanwhile, Harrisburg "lost" $600,000 over the previous 20 years. The chamber of commerce noted that 700 businesses left the city between 1969 and 1975 (Beers).

As the saying goes, you get the government you deserve. And in the decade before the 80s, Harrisburg elected a Mayor who was famous for running his own small business into the ground. I'm sure when he won you could sense a collective suburbanite sigh—followed by a melodramatic eye roll.

It is worth noting, some did try to help. A Methodist mission once came to Harrisburg, but left saying, "It is one of the most depressed and deteriorated communities I have ever seen—houses in disrepair, crowded, dirty street" (Beers).

Harrisburg had developed such a terrible reputation that no new cities were established in the 20th or 21st century in central Pennsylvania. Suburbanites rejected what Harrisburg had become to such an extent, they wouldn't be caught dead living in a city. Instead, they preferred to call their communities towns, boroughs and villages.

As if not wanting to live in a dirty, broke and deteriorating place wasn't bad enough, it was also in the 70s that a nuclear reactor 13 miles south of the city had a near meltdown that garnered international headlines for weeks. The almost-crisis at Three Mile Island was the product of human error. Fortunately, a real blown crisis was averted by precautions that worked. Yes, 133 tons of uranium fuel threatened a possible meltdown. Yes, millions of lives were at risk. But ultimately, a crisis didn't happen and no one immediately died. Yet, to this day, those vapor spewing stacks in the middle of the Susquehanna River serve as a mile high reminder of what is possible. And, in reality, if this was going to happen anywhere and at any time, why not Harrisburg and why not the 1970s?

With the city steadfastly dying, Harrisburg residents enthusiastically voted in a 1970 referendum for a "strong-mayor" form of government, which is typically reserved for larger cities. Harrisburgers decided to increasingly put their fortunes in the hands of one person. And that one person would come a decade later and take that "strong-mayor" government to new heights.

Side note: When crews were fixing the giant sinkhole on North Fourth, it proved to be a bit larger than expected. As a backhoe was removing debris from the bottom of the initial hole, it expanded, swallowing the giant machine. The vision made for great TV, although it did prolong the suffering for those waiting to return home.

9: CITY OF UNREST

WHEN STEPHEN RUSSELL REED was elected mayor in 1981, he held an inaugural ball and called for a "New Generation." This tradition of grand parties following ballot victories endured throughout all seven terms. For the finale in 2006, 500 people gladly paid $50 a ticket to eat and drink with the man who would be named the world's third best mayor. It was held in the luxurious Hilton Harrisburg—one of Reed's finest achievements. During this final ball, I was working in Wyoming and had never heard of Mayor Reed. So, I wasn't there. But, I'd bet a few paychecks no one was calling for another "New Generation"—after all, by definition Reed had been mayor for nearly one-and-a-half.

It's hard to accurately explain how dead Harrisburg was when Reed took over. I can continue to give you all the statistics about blight, abandoned homes and median income. I could tell you all about how HUD named Harrisburg one of the nation's most distressed cities in 1980. But to honestly illustrate the state of the city during that time would take an entire chapter bloated with dreary detail. Instead, I'll just give you a few figures. The first is 30 percent. That's about the average voter turnout for a mayoral election in Pennsylvania's capital city. Compare that to a 78 percent Harrisburg turnout in the 2008 presidential election. Either way, the people are electing a CEO. But one is clearly viewed as more important. Over the past few decades, a significant majority of voters in Harrisburg have shown they just don't care about local politics.

That's why Reed's victory in 1981 was so impressive. Despite his age of 32, he had already served three terms in the State Legislature and one as county commissioner. He earned such a reputation that his magic number was thought to be '84, the first election for which he was eligible for president. By running for mayor—a job many thought beneath him—he put his political career in jeopardy.

With such low voter turnout, trends are hard to calculate. Yet, Reed managed to continue his streak of ballot success by dethroning the incumbent mayor in the primaries by garnering nearly 9,000 votes—or well over double his nearest opponent. Given the expectations surrounding his future, many wondered why he would want to be mayor of a bombed out city when his political career would surely end in the White House.

After Reed's first inaugural ball, he quickly got to work by slashing the recent increases in property taxes, thus instilling some confidence in the city's remaining residents. One of his major early achievements was his use of what is known as a Land Value Taxation. I understand that sounds boring, but it's important. An LVT is a type of property tax. The concept is to tax land at a high rate and tax improvements to that land at a lower rate. Most property taxes assess the entire value of the land. By placing a lower tax on improvements, land owners are more willing to invest in their properties. This concept is popular around the globe, but rare in America. When Reed took office there was estimated to be more than 4,200 vacant buildings in Harrisburg's downtown. That quickly dropped to less than 500. While the LVT actually took effect before Reed was elected, its most visible success happened under his watch. Thus, he was seen as an immediate winner—a mayor who could get results. He quickly began to earn the trust of the people— a type of trust where most assumed he was governing in the right.

I could take a few more paragraphs and list Reed's early and lasting accomplishments from upstart businesses to new museums and from crime reduction to city revenues. But here's the gist. In the decade preceding his election, the city lost 22 percent of its population. In the first decade of his reign, it lost just 1.7 percent. By 2010, his final decade in office, the population increased for the first time since 1950. When he left office in 2010, a decline in populace returned.

An optimist, Reed had an acute passion for politics. He won every election he ever entered, except his last. His smile made you smile. His laugh made you laugh. He was so adored, it's rumored an antique shop in Tucson, Arizona placed him in its hall of fame after he visited.

At 5'9", he physically intimidated no one. Yet, no matter the topic, he professed a believable expertise. His well-crafted media image directly opposed his executive style. He ran Harrisburg as if it were New York City or Chicago. Though, in public, he possessed the ability to turn a crowded room into an intimate setting.

But during the later parts of his second decade in power his short-sighted vision for improvements began to show—as did his ruthless thirst for power. And for the first time, his mayoral decisions came under scrutiny— albeit a relatively small amount. It was these years, the 90s into the early 2000s, where my reporting focused. Those were the years that told the story of the real Stephen Reed—the one few knew, or just simply ignored.

Reed's tenure lasted from his early 30s to his 60s. During such a span, any human would necessarily evolve in personality, temperament and countenance. For Reed, perhaps it was the scintilla of disapproval he did receive.

Perhaps his workaholic nature, of late nights and early mornings, had worn on him. Perhaps it was the pressure to continue his string of stunning urban successes. But not matter the cause, by his regime's third decade, the Mayor had grown reclusive. A bizarre mystique of heavy drinking and chain-smoking surrounded his new persona. Gestapo-like control tactics involving pre-approval of newspaper stories were heavily rumored. Also rumored were romantic trysts with certain male newspaper reporters. Reed's sexuality was well-known, and accepted.

As much as he was public, he had matured to be equally as private. Many began to lose sight of who he was. Others questioned if they ever really knew him at all.

Yet, despite whatever creature he became, few would suggest he quit caring about the people. He was an astrologically accurate Leo with no college degree, spouse or children. Three things he would never obtain, meaning the city received all his attention. If there was a murder, he was on scene to calm the residents. If a fired ripped through a row home, he would assess the damage and address the media. He was hands on. And in his hands the city felt comfortable. He was a mayor of unrest. And that unrest was greatly missed when he relinquished the office.

If you talk to police officers in Harrisburg, they will tell you the excitement level in the city increases with the temperature. So was the case on May 11, 2011. It had been a tough winter and this was the best day followed by the best night of the year. The type of weather when the breeze is warm, but the sun is not too hot—though the shade of the sunset is welcomed.

It was around 8:15 in the evening. I was sitting at my desk preparing my story for that night's 10:00 o'clock news. I had my interviews and my video. The story was written and my photographer was just about finished editing. It was quiet. Then, the scanners began to scream.

"Shots fired! Shots fired! Man down!"

Emergency sirens in the background largely drowned out the distress calls. The distorted nature of the officer's urgency gripped our attention. I rushed to the scanner table to listen more closely. The assignment desk manager did the same.

"We have multiple gunshot wounds. Suspect spotted on the run. Crews in pursuit."

The scanner then went dead. Listening to scanner traffic is awful. It's like putting together an incomplete puzzle without having the picture on the box to help. You rarely get all the information you need. Newsroom decisions are oftentimes made via certain language and perceived distress levels. Then, of course, you have to make sure it's not a drill.

"We have about a dozen gun shots," the scanner shrieked back to life.

One officer fought to speak while on foot pursuit. "I see the suspect. I'm closing in."

Another officer yelled over the howl of an approaching ambulance. "We have a large crowd around the victim."

"What is your location?" Dispatch was far calmer.

"500 block of McClay. Send backup. I need backup!"

My desk manager and I shared a glimpse.

"Alex!" I yelled for my photographer. "Grab your shit, we need to go."

The shooting was only a few blocks from the station. As our rusty truck squeaked to a stop, the victim was still lying on the ground. You could tell emergency crews had been working on him for a while. They had him largely wrapped and lying on a folded gurney. Blood-seeped bandages concealed his most severe injuries. I'm sure he was given some type of sedative, but with every breath he grimaced.

My photographer jumped out of the truck with his gear. I pulled out my phone and got what video I could. Hundreds of restless onlookers crowded around the police tape, which was doing a lousy job of keeping them back. Within a minute of our arrival, with dozens of locals immediately surrounding the victim, the medics erected the gurney and loaded him into the ambulance. As the wheels rolled, the victim bounced along the uneven walkway. I could hear the man moan—while his loved ones succumbed to tears.

Police allowed a few people to rush up and place a gentle hand or offer a loving word. Meanwhile, others were clearly more pissed than passive. As the rear ambulance door shut, the lights turned on. With a quick scream from the siren the young black man was whisked off to the hospital.

"I don't like this." My photog looked up from his camera. He was getting shots of the shell casings scattered in front of the home. Police numbered each and then snapped their own photos. I counted at least a dozen.

"Yeah," I replied quietly. "I don't think we should stay long."

About 15 police officers remained on scene to asked questions and collect evidence. Meanwhile, the hundreds of locals that gathered showed no signs of leaving or sedating. Their eyes were set with un-repose. And given what they had just witnessed, it appeared they were ripe to recoil.

"Get your video, fast," I said. "I'll see what info I can get. When the police leave, we leave."

The block we were on was your typical low-income, Section 8 housing. The homes were simple, repetitive, brick squares, lined close to the streets. No shutters. Few trees. Some bushes. Mostly, it was just dead weeds and jagged sidewalks. Getting around entailed the concentration to dodge McDonalds cups and Philly Blunt wrappers.

"What happened?" I approached one of the officers I knew. Harrisburg police were notorious for not releasing information publicly. At a normal police department, the position of public information officer (PIO) is to talk to the media and inform the public. Harrisburg's PIO is the only one I ever worked with in my career that refused to go on camera. Getting him to return an email with more than one sentence was noteworthy. I had been told it was the typical Reed policy holdover. Silence breeds corruption.

"I didn't tell you any of this," the officer responded.

I nodded. Despite the department's lack of transparency, many of the officers and detectives would give information, anonymously.

The officer told me the victim got into a gunfight with another man. About a dozen shots were fired, and some of the rounds ended up in the victim's arm and leg. After the shooting, the suspect, a young black man, took off and was quickly arrested. One gun was recovered. More likely than not, multiple gunmen were involved. The challenge for police was finding someone willing to talk.

"How much longer do you think you'll be here?" I asked the officer.

"Not too much longer," he replied. "Five, ten minutes."

As we were talking, the crowd continued to grow in numbers and attitude. Like tributaries into a river, the alleys just seemed to leak an endless flow of vocal residents.

"Locals seem a little restless," I added.

"It's the first beautiful evening of the year." He smiled. "Things should be interesting for the next few months."

The officer walked away as my photographer walked up.

"You have all you need?" I asked.

He nodded, his eyes cautiously fixed on a section of the crowd that seemed more agitated than the rest.

"Police are about to leave," I mentioned, looking at the same group as he was. "Let's pack up."

In the higher crime sections of the city, station policy was "leave with the police." But like most aspects of my life, words carry far less meaning than experience. So, when I first arrived in Harrisburg, I ignored that rule. I'll admit my focus on journalism overruled my common sense. It was stupid and I quickly learned my lesson.

On the day in which I learned this lesson, I happened to be with the same photographer covering another shooting in a depressed area of the city. After the police left, I wanted to go live at the scene for the 10 and 11 o'clock news. My photog tried hard to convince me otherwise.

"What are you afraid of?" I asked him.

"The ghetto, late at night," he bemoaned.

I mentally logged his concerns, but ultimately ignored them. We did that 10 o'clock hit at the scene of the shooting. And you know what? We had the best live shot of the night. Being on scene, I was able to show viewers exactly what happened. All the other stations went live from the safety of the police station downtown.

"Wimps," I thought to myself.

So there we were, 10:30 at night, sitting inside a live truck in one of the worst sections of—statistically—one of the most dangerous cities in America. From my previous ghetto live shot experience, I knew this was about the time neighborhoods became active. Up until 10:30 things are usually pretty quiet. But by 10:30, that begins to change as the front doors begin to creak open.

By 10:35, the porches are usually full. The periodic flash of BIC lighters reveal how full. Noise is rare. But stares are common. It's obvious no one wants us there.

The streets are just as dark as the porches. Any light bulbs Harrisburg can afford to replace usually illuminate higher income areas. *Fortunately* for us, the shooting happened near one of the few working light posts. At the time, it seemed like the best place to avoid trouble. Looking back, we only succeeded in making ourselves brighter targets.

During this time, I kept my eyes buried in a book. But I'd be a liar if I said I didn't occasionally glance upward.

Then, suddenly, we felt it.

BOOM!!!

"Shit!" We both yelled! Our bodies jolted awake. "What the hell was that!?"

The shock reverberated through the hollow truck like a M-80.

Then another.

BOOM!!!

Both objects hit near the same spot towards the rear of the van.

"F***!!" My photographer yelled, "We're under attack!!"

The force of the second hit rocked the truck back and forth. From the inside, I could see the van's thin metal shell had two dents on the driver's side.

"What the hell are they throwing at us?" My voice was probably much higher and more panicked than I remember. "Rocks?"

"Maybe." Alex scanned his side view mirror. "I don't know. I don't see anything."

Normally, we would have just slammed the truck in "D" and took off. But we were tethered to all our equipment outside: lights, tripod, camera, electrical cords, and coaxial cable. If we drove off, it was coming with us. We were stuck.

I quickly dialed the station's number, when we got hit again. This time, an apple exploded against the driver's side door glass. Had the window been down, my photographer would have taken a direct hit by a high velocity Red Delicious.

"Fruit," he hollered. "They're throwing fruit at us!"

"Hey!" The desk answered. "We're under attack!" I tried not to act too startled—just enough for them to get the point. "You might be on your own for the 11:00."

"Alex," I looked over at my photog. By this point, he had punched the automatic door locks about five times. "They want you to get out and pack the stuff. We can leave."

His eyes widened. "I'm not getting out of this truck. You do it. You're the dumb ass that wanted to stay here."

"Don't blame this shit on me," I yelled back. "Plus, I can't get out. I'm in a suit. Fruit will stain it."

With a look of profound disgust, he pulled out his phone and started scrolling.

"What are you doing?" I asked.

"Calling the cops," he condescendingly replied.

It turned out an officer we knew was only a few blocks away.

"I hear the local boys are having some fun with you guys." We didn't roll down the window until we could read the name on his badge. "Why are you guys even here?"

My photog rolled his eyes. Needless to say, that was the last time I stayed on a scene in the ghetto after the police left.

So, when police were wrapping up their investigation on McClay Street after the man was shot in the arm and leg, I was ready to go. But what happened next, would keep us there a bit longer.

It had now been a few minutes since the ambulance carried off the victim. Police had arrested that one gunman and were trying to learn of more. But the residents were not being talkative—especially with so many of their community members watching.

The longer the cops stayed, the more restless the locals became. Using racial slurs and epithets, they made it very clear, they did not want the law there, or us. As a journalist, covering mass movements of agitated people is exacting. The feat of balancing safety with performance flows with each moment. Sometimes you make the right call. Sometimes you don't. But ultimately, the outcome is mostly determined by what those around you are willing to allow. And on this day, those around us didn't appear forgiving.

Next to the cops, my photographer and I were the only white people in sight. We were about 30 minutes in, and other media still had not arrived. Had they been there, I would have felt a little more secure. More cameras mean more coverage and theoretically more protection. But we were on our own.

"If Mayor Reed were mayor, he'd be here to fix this shit." I heard one woman yell.

"Where's Thompson at?" hollered another. "Where's the sister? We got issues here in the hood."

Cries for the police to leave were growing more frequent and more emphatic.

I could feel the energy of the people begin to consolidate. What had been a collection of shifting grievances began to form into a singular mindset. And we found ourselves surrounded, a block away from the relative safety of our truck. There would be no quick escape.

The increased level of agitation manifested into an increased level of clamor. Talking became yelling. Standing became shuffling. Walking became running. We were increasingly being circled by thicker rows. Our camera made us a focus that offered a legitimate pathway to exposure. I just got a feeling that something was about to happen.

I grabbed my photographer by the elbow as he filmed off his shoulder. "Whatever happens, keep recording."

Like waves of a curtain, the crowd began to move in unison. We tried to stand our ground, but were forced to sway along.

"F*** the police," the cries began.

"You best get out, white boys," others voiced. "This ain't your hood."

Amongst the commotion, off to the right, I heard a quick fit of sheer panic. Like a middle school fight, scores of aroused denizens had formed a circle around something.

"Come on!" I worked to clear a path for my photographer. It was a far easier task than I had anticipated. The crowd willingly parted.

When we reached a clearing, a large black man with dreads was physically engaged with a policeman. With clenched jaws and arched backs, they clawed and wrestled for the upper hand. But what was one cop quickly became three, then four. With no one in the crowd coming to the man's aid, he was quickly overpowered, spun and pressed hard against a wall.

"Now you know what the F*** it is to stay in this life!" He hollered while being cuffed—his face pressed against the siding. "Mother F*****!"

With the man subdued, the crowd shifted its attention to other men, not yet cuffed—but soon to be. The situation was quickly getting out of control. The cops were outnumbered 20 to 1. You could sense the growing empowerment of the majority. Common sense told me to get the hell out of there, but my news instinct wouldn't allow it.

Thankfully, my nerves were for not. When the German Shepherds arrived, the crowd immediately calmed, quieted and dispersed. I had never witnessed such a drastic adjustment of priorities. On numerous occasions in the ghetto, I've been told by residents how honor is bestowed upon those who fight cops. Win or lose, the brave are lionized—especially by the young. But there's absolutely no honor is being ripped apart by an 85-pound animal.

Later than night, at the police station, I talked to an older neighbor lady who wanted to give police some information. She told me anonymously, "All these people doing all this shooting and being locked up. Instead, we need to send them to Iraq. They want to fight. They need to go over and fight the war. Let's see how brave they are then."

This was the closest I have ever been to a riot. But the same cannot be said for Harrisburg.

In June of 1969, the racial tensions that had engulfed America finally made it to central Pennsylvania—a place where racial lines had been drawn decades earlier. Those lines separated income, education and crime. But up until 1969, conditions had yet to devolve into violence.

The riot kicked off after a black school teacher tried to buy cigarettes, but the manager said the store was closed. One violent week later, an 18-year-old Harrisburg High School student was dead. He had been shot and killed by a city police officer who claimed the young man was in the process of lighting a Molotov cocktail. In the chaos, 15

others were wounded, 103 were arrested and eight structures were arsoned. Other news reports cited shattered
windows, vandalized cars and damaged merchandise.

This was not the Watts riots or other significant racial
disturbances around the county, so it didn't received the
subsequent attention. But it did serve to scare the hell
out of people in the Susquehanna Valley. What few
privileged residents remained in the city at that point,
fled. By 1976, Harrisburg's Mayor observed the city was
losing its "well-to-do younger, more productive segments
of its population, leaving the cities a high proportion of
the old, the poor and the minorities, who cannot afford or
are not allowed similar freedom of movement" (Beers).

The 1969 riot marked the first instance of direct racial
hostility in central Pennsylvania and the state's capital.
The races were always separated by geography and
quality of life, but now they were separated by an ideology
of intolerance. Nearly 20,000 whites vanished from
Harrisburg in the 1970s. The school district was on its
way to becoming a nearly all-minority district. By 1982, it
was 80 percent.

Harrisburg had officially gone to newcomers. Nobody
else wanted it.

Behold the infamous incinerator.

An abandoned city block; partially collapsed building; rusted out fire hydrant; and overgrown sidewalk. All this, just blocks away from a billion dollar Capitol complex.

A row of boarded up houses three blocks from the Capitol dome. During the day, state workers occupy the parking spots. At night, drug addicts climb in through the broken windows seeking shelter.

My live shot the night of October 11, 2011 when City Council filed for
bankruptcy.

Harrisburg City Council convenes days after its vote to declare
bankruptcy. With the community sounding off, one Council member
(who voted yes) apparently didn't find it necessary to show up.

Harrisburg City Council bankruptcy attorney, Mark Schwartz. As of the publishing of this book, he still hadn't been paid $290,000 in legal bills he charged to the city. In late 2013, he sued.

Among his many impressive achievements as mayor, many consider the National Civil War Museum among Mayor Stephen Reed's finest.

As of this book's publishing, Dan Miller still argues bankruptcy was Harrisburg's best option for a lasting recovery - an option he feels will someday become a necessity.

Mayor Linda Thompson taking a media question (possibly from me) following the unveiling of her Act 47 financial recovery plan.

A confident and beloved Mayor Stephen R. Reed being sworn in as Harrisburg's Mayor in 1982. He proudly answered the call to serve.

Harrisburg Communications Director Bob Philbin and I conversing at the giant sinkhole on North 4th Street.

10: RISING TIDES

FOR PENNSYLVANIA'S CAPITAL CITY, 2011 was a hot mess. Professionally, I have never been involved in anything so disorganized, so chaotic and so unfortunate. In the closing days of the previous year, after first applying, the capital was granted status into—what is known as—Act 47. Harrisburg became the 20th "distressed" state municipality to be active in the program. Under the simplest of propagandized terms, under Act 47, the state provides an economic adviser to draft a financial recovery plan for the troubled municipality. Low interest or zero interest loans, technical assistance and other benefits are also available.

The day Act 47 was granted, many rejoiced. "The City of Harrisburg is economically distressed. This is an important first step on the city's road to fiscal recovery. There will be difficult choices to be made by the city's leaders as we craft a comprehensive long term recovery plan," said Mayor Thompson.

"For us in this situation, it is a positive step and more directly, right now we are dealing with the budget for 2011 and it doesn't seem like the Thompson administration is willing to make those hard decisions. So, I'm hoping an Act 47 coordinator will come in and force us to actually do that," snipped the "homosexual, evil little" city Controller.

The concept of Act 47 was devised in 1987 to provide a safety net for distressed cities and municipalities in the Commonwealth. I found it odd that a state bloated with corruption and billions in debt was called in to "rescue" a city bloated with corruption and millions in debt, but I digress. The point is no city ever accepted into the program has gotten out. The rational for why has been debated ad nauseam.

It works like this, the Department of Community and Economic Development studies the city's books, assesses its assets and drafts a recovery plan that merrily solves all the problems. It's true, most of the recovery plans for the various cities are so similar it can be argued a general template is used—but I digress again. The mighty government of the sixth largest state in the union has arrived—all is right.

So, as went the plan, the state came in with a slew of brilliant economic advisers. They studied the books, assessed the assets and drafted a recovery plan. Up to this point, everyone was on board: the state, City Council and Mayor—together in uncomfortable unison.

But, the tenuous peace collapsed when the state's plan was released in July of 2011. In part, the plan called for the selling of city assets, the raising of property taxes, and elimination of city workers while calling for cuts in salaries and benefits. Out of this original Act 47 plan, a majority of City Council known as the "gang of four" emerged. It was these four part-time, small-city, officials that would eventually hold hostage the most powerful financial and political institutions in the world.

When the state originally drafted Act 47, it wasn't designed to be a complete state takeover. City Council and the Mayor still had to approve the financial recovery plan. Given the dire situation that led to the city's need for Act 47 status, and the state's benevolence, it was probably never assumed that any plan would be rejected. But in

July of 2011, by a vote of 4-3, Harrisburg City Council became the first municipality in the state's history to reject the recovery plan crafted for it.

I said that night on air during my report, "I just want to make this clear, this has never happened before. So right now, Harrisburg has a debt of $310 million, which is six times its budget. Its debtors are suing it and it's projected to run out of money by the fourth quarter of this year. And now it has no plan on the table for recovery."

"This was not a global solution," said one Council member the night of the vote. "This didn't count for all parties to have a significant contribution. This is not the shared pain we are looking for."

Mayor Thompson took charge. "The first thing I'm going to do tomorrow is reach out to our creditors to calm and stabilize the markets to ensure them that I plan on having a plan prepared given the deadline I am given." The following day, despite her noble efforts, the markets failed to calm.

This Act 47 process up to this point had cost the state taxpayers $600,000. With that "no" vote the money was essentially wasted. Plus, remember, the city asked the state for Act 47 protection. The state didn't come to the city. But city officials recognized Harrisburg's financial troubles were too big for them to handle.

Under the provisions of the act, the Mayor now had 14 days to submit her own recovery plan. By this time, such a schism had developed between Council and the Mayor they had ceased talking. All correspondence happened through the media. Like a pack of trained dogs, the press would scurry through the atrium, between Council chambers and the Mayor's office, to get reaction to what each had just said about the other. The Mayor would slam City Council for being stubborn and failing to provide its own recovery plan. The "gang of four" would then call into question the Mayor's competence.

That night, they would each watch the media reports to see what the other said. The next day, the process would start over. I had never been involved in anything so absurd.

So, naturally, when the Mayor presented her plan, it had no chance of passing. Thompson basically put the state's plan on an office machine and hit copy. To her credit, she was able to secure some concessions from the county and state, but not nearly enough. Council promptly rejected her plan 4-3. But not before a contentious Council session, which the Mayor refused to attend, where the black women on Council yelled at, interrupted and verbally assaulted each other.

"She's going to respect this committee and be an adult," rudely snipped Council President to a member of the "gang of four." The "gang" member was snickering and whispering as Council President addressed the chamber. Council President was one of Thompson's few political supporters and the "gang" had little respect for her positions.

"This is a new place where no other city has ever been and I think this is a new opportunity to re-start that dialogue," one of the "gang" members told me. "The plan that was put out by the Mayor was untenable and the numbers didn't work for the city. And it was one we could not feel comfortable passing. There was no global solution, no shared pain."

Those were the buzz terms: "global solution" and "shared pain." It wasn't just the city that dug this hole. The "gang of four" felt the bond insurers, state, and county should all "share" in a painful solution. Up to this point, all the pain was placed on the impoverished city taxpayers. Meanwhile, the billionaires on Wall Street who issued the inexplicable debt were getting paid in full. Council found that unacceptable.

It was also on this day, when the Mayor's plan was rejected, that the calls for a new direction emerged.

"I do think we need to take action, now," the city Controller told me when I called him about Thompson's failed plan. "I don't think we should be waiting any longer. But, the debt just continues to pile up. What I would like to see Council do now is hire a lawyer and give them the authority to declare bankruptcy."

It was also at this time, the possibility of a complete takeover was discussed.

"Why take away the peoples' right to have representation, because they [gang of four] want to sit here and be petty?" asked Council President. "We went to the state and asked for the Act 47 intervention plan. We're asking for this."

It was also on this night, my relationship with Mayor Thompson took a drastic turn. After her recovery plan was rejected, the media shuffled around Council chambers getting comment for our stories. Meanwhile, the Mayor was preparing her media room for the rush. When the time came, the media assembled around the atrium elevators en-route to the second floor. The first elevator was full, so I waited for the second. From the first floor, via the open atrium, I could hear the elevator open and let my colleagues out on the second. It then returned for me.

When I got to the second floor, the media had just started entering the Mayor's pressroom. My photographer and I joined the back of the line and followed the slow progression. As we approached the door, I saw the city's Communications Director inside. I was getting ready to chat it up with him, but after the person in front of me walked in, he shut the door. I then heard a click.

"What the hell?" I reached down to turn the knob. Locked. I looked up at my photographer. "What just happened?"

I grabbed the handle again and shook it. Then shook it once more. I couldn't believe it. This was a huge night. The city was collapsing. Council just shot down another recovery plan. And the Mayor just locked me out of her office. Given her proclivity for memorable sound bites, I was at great risk of being beaten by all my peers.

In the weeks prior to this vote, I had done a series of stories with which Thompson apparently was not happy. The pieces were not particularly flattering to her, but they were not unreasonably critical, either.

Maybe that was it. Maybe she just didn't want me in there. Thompson and I always had a contemptuous relationship. I was one of the few reporters willing to directly challenge her at press conferences. I knew she didn't like it. But that's how I got my best sound bites.

"I can't believe it," I uttered to my photog. "Fine! She wants to play games. I can play games."

So, I balled my hand into the tightest fist I could and began pounding on the door. In straight succession, I laid a barrage of attacks on the hardwood. I gave it a minute; no answer. So, I started pounding again. Harrisburg city hall has a multi-story open atrium. My frustrations echoed throughout the entire damn thing. The longer the door stayed locked, the more motivated I became. I pounded on that door until my knuckles grew sore. I then rotated my hand to use the soft underside of my fist.

The Mayor's presser lasted about 15 minutes. I didn't knock the entire time. I didn't want to be too obnoxious. But we stood next to the door until we heard it unlock. Instinctively, my hand snatched the knob, turned and pushed.

"Start recording and don't stop," I told my photog.

When it opened, the Mayor's Communications Director was blocking the entryway.

"What the hell, Bob!" I blurted out. Behind him, my media colleagues were packing their equipment. They all ignored me.

"Where's the Mayor, Bob?" I was pissed. "I want my interview. I want it now! Where's the Mayor?" I looked beyond him towards the podium.

He put his hands up to stop my advance. Though he was careful not to touch me. I had 6 inches, 50 pounds and 25 years on Bob. He had no desire to further piss me off. "The Mayor is done answering media questions for the night. She has retired to her chambers."

"Didn't you hear me knocking out here?" I asked rhetorically. There was no way they didn't. The whole damn building heard me.

"We didn't hear anything," he said. "We didn't hear you knocking. You were late to the meeting and we shut the door."

"The Mayor's 45 minutes late for everything," I replied forcefully. "Fine," I took a breath. "Then, will you answer my questions?"

He nodded.

I can't even remember what I asked him or what he said in reply. My questions were simply an attempt to inconvenience him. If Thompson was trying to send me a message, it was delivered. And it only motivated me further. It's a shame she couldn't communicate that effectively all the time.

A few weeks after Thompson locked me out of that press conference, a third version of a recovery plan was rejected by City Council. By this point, the feud between Thompson and Council reach a point where they would barely mention each other by name. The state was also out of ideas. The process for Act 47 had been exhausted. As I said, no city had ever rejected the recovery plan. Harrisburg had now rejected three. So, the PA Legislature quickly wrote and passed legislation to simply appoint a receiver and take the city over.

Suburban legislators had harsh words for their Harrisburg counterparts.

"To me it doesn't make any sense," said one local state Senator who called City Council's efforts reckless and irresponsible. "My sense is they're looking for a bailout. They are looking for somebody else to pay for their irresponsibility over the years. And that's just not going to happen."

County commissioners released this statement: "We are extremely disappointed that a majority of City Council has again failed to take any action to resolve the financial condition of the city. The county will continue to pursue its remedies in the interest of all county taxpayers." What they failed to mention in the statement is that the county was largely to blame for the problem and is on the hook for the failures. The county owned $140 million in Harrisburg's debt for guaranteeing many of the loans that ruined the city. Now, they wanted all their money and none of the responsibility. The same mentality was found on Wall Street. That is what Council was fighting.

Other city leaders, not on Council, explained to me why the recovery plans were bad for the city. Even if Harrisburg sold all its assets, which the plans suggested, there wouldn't be enough money to pay the debt. And without those assets, city revenues would decline. Years down the road, Harrisburg would find itself back near the brink of bankruptcy. So, it made sense for Council to reject the plans and force the state to further intervene and accept accountability for the inevitable failure.

Politically, Council understood its position. The state couldn't allow Harrisburg to fail for fear of a catastrophic reaction within the financial markets. If Pennsylvania isn't willing to save its own capital city, how could creditors be assured their loans would be safe in any Commonwealth city or municipality?

These tensions between the main players stifled discussion. Nobody wanted to talk to anybody about anything of significance. You just got the feeling all was lost. Meanwhile, the city was running out of money to service any of its debt or pay its employees. It had resorted to buying time with the sale on tax liens, early collections of debt payments or taking out loans with outrageous interest rates. But these stop gaps only provided enough money to honor payroll. Soon, Harrisburg would default on its General Obligation Debt and the service of much of the Reed debt halted. I quit counting the lawsuits when I ran out of fingers and toes. Every day the hole got bigger.

As the city continued to flounder, I decided to do some digging into its financial records. I just had a hunch there was more to the story that what we were being told. In the closing months of 2011, I released the following reports detailing Harrisburg's "Hidden Debt." Keep in mind all this was happening in the latter half of 2011 when the national economy was struggling.

Here is the first report with the text and how it appeared in the teleprompter for air. Feel free to read it as if you were a newsman.

Anchor Intro:

We start with the Capital City in Crisis and a CBS 21 exclusive. As if Harrisburg's financial situation wasn't bad enough, we have uncovered new information showing that Harrisburg taxpayers are on the hook for more money— big money. And you may not even know about it. CBS 21's Chris Papst is live with the Dauphin County Mobile Newsroom in Harrisburg and Chris you are the first reporter on this and it's a staggering amount of money.

Papst Intro from Center City:

Robb, we're talking about a $100 million here. We found this hidden debt just hanging over the city's head and it's connected to a project to improve the city's downtown shopping district, Strawberry Square. And it's something that is not being discussed and it's not dealt with in any of the financial recovery plans.

Package Report:

It was at a time when the economy was strong and money was flowing. It was the late 90s, and a local contractor, Harristown Development, wanted to fix up Strawberry Square, so they turned to the city for help.

The Harrisburg Redevelopment Authority was heavily involved in the project and under Mayor Stephen Reed the city guaranteed substantial loans totaling nearly $24 million in 1998. But with interest the total loan amount could reach $95 million. And what Harristown Development cannot pay, Harrisburg would have to pick up.

Dan Miller: Harrisburg Controller

"It's just another potential sword hanging over our heads. It's there. It's real and it's $95 million."

This is similar to the incinerator where the city guaranteed hundreds of millions of dollars in loans it can't pay back.

Dan Miller: Harrisburg Controller

"We already have a large deficit. So any amount is going to make that deficit larger. And we can't pay it."

Reporter Tag:

We are not speculating that Harristown Development won't be able to pay the loan back. But a few weeks ago, I was at a City Council meeting, and a representative from Strawberry Square pleaded with City Council not to raise parking fees, because Strawberry Square has lost clients lately and another big one is leaving at the end of this year.

Anchor Question:

When is this $95 million due?

Papst Answer:

Not all at once. The big question here is what happens in 2016 when the payments on the loans jump from $75,000 a year to millions. And if Harristown Development cannot pay that money, Harrisburg will have to and it could total $95 million.

END SCRIPT

Harristown didn't return my calls for the story until after it aired. I was offered this obligatory statement by the vice-president, "We're like everyone else in this economy; it's been a tough couple of years. We're meeting all our obligations; we continue to put together leasing deals. We have new tenants coming in. We continue to be optimistic about the future in this economy."

We called Mayor Thompson's office for comment on this debt, but she didn't know this money was due.

Here's the second "Hidden Debt" story:

Anchor Intro:

Now to the Capital City in Crisis and a story you will only see on CBS 21. The state asked for it and now it gets it. Harrisburg is in even more financial trouble than first thought. Now, as the state prepares to take over, CBS 21 has learned of a massive public works project mandated by the EPA to clean up the Susquehanna River. And the city doesn't have the money to do it. CBS 21's Chris Papst is live with the Dauphin County Mobile Newsroom in Harrisburg and Chris, much like the story you did on the possible Strawberry Square debt, this isn't getting any attention either.

Papst Intro from Center City:

No, and we are talking a $70 million project here. Marc Kurowski, the Chairman of the Harrisburg Authority, which owns the sewage plant, told me today this should be a huge story, but it's getting overshadowed by the other financial issues in the city.

Package Report:

When the state takes over Harrisburg it will have a lot to handle. Such as $310 million in incinerator debt, a budget deficit, shrinking revenue, numerous lawsuits, union contracts and a City Council that is pushing for bankruptcy. And now you can add one more huge problem to that list.

Marc Kurowski: Chairman: Harrisburg Authority

"This was something that has been coming for years because of the Chesapeake Bay and other regulatory requirement."

A few years ago, the EPA issued new pollution rules for wastewater treatment plants. It's designed to help clean the Chesapeake Bay. Harrisburg's plant is the largest on the Susquehanna River in Pennsylvania and does not meet the new requirements. And the price tag to meet them: $70 million.

Marc Kurowski: Chairman: Harrisburg Authority

"The bottom line is we need the funding. That's the issue."

And right now, the funding simply isn't there. The city has no money and with the current financial crisis taking out a loan would be a long shot. Construction is scheduled to begin as early as spring. Some hope when the state takes over, it will offer help.

Marc Kurowski: Chairman: Harrisburg Authority

"It seems like a reasonable option considering it is the capital of Pennsylvania, as we go, in some ways, so goes the state."

"Are we going to work with a state receiver if they come into play? Absolutely, this is a big discussion we'll have with them because this is something we have to figure out."

"It's only going to continue to become more pressing."

Papst Outcue:

I called the EPA, but they did not seem very sympathetic to Harrisburg's situation. They want the treatment plant upgraded. If it doesn't happen the city will have to buy pollution credits to offset the failure to meet the requirements. So either way city taxpayers are going to have to pay. Or, as it may be, state taxpayers— since the state did decide to take this situation over.
END SCRIPT

And the third "Hidden Debt" report:

Anchor Intro:

And now to the Capital City in Crisis and a CBS 21 news exclusive. It appears Harrisburg's financial future is even more dire than anyone thought. CBS 21 has uncovered more hidden debt and this one could make you angry. CBS 21's Chris Papst is live with the Dauphin County Mobile Newsroom in Harrisburg and Chris, how much money are we talking here?

Papst Intro from Center City:

This is an astounding amount: $184 million. Much like the other hidden debts we've uncovered here on CBS 21—the Strawberry Square debt and sewage plant upgrades—this is not dealt with in any of the city's recovery plans. The other two were at least mentioned in the recovery plans. This $184 million is nowhere to be found.

Package Report:

When people think Harrisburg financial crisis, most think incinerator. And while that debt is huge, it's just the beginning. Did you ever hear the term, OPEB? It stands for Other Post-Employment Benefits. Basically, when someone retires from the city, they not only get a pension, they get these OPEBs, which cover healthcare. In 2008, an OPEB study found Harrisburg owes its future retirees an astounding $184 million.

Dan Miller: City Controller

"How big of a deal is this? This is huge. Why is it getting no attention? Because it's not being felt right now."

But it soon will be felt, and in a big way. According to the study, Harrisburg should be paying 18 million every year to fully fund these OPEBs for the future. But the city can only afford about $4.5 million, which is what it owes current retirees. So the liability for all future retirees is $184 million. And eventually Harrisburg will have to pay it.

Dan Miller: City Controller

"We're not going to have any money to pay it. The benefits have to be put in line with what, not only the city can afford, but what is going on in the private sector."

This debt is so hidden the people affected most don't even know about it. Eric Jenkins, the president of the firefighters union gave us this statement. "That would be a concern that the benefits would not be there to cover our guys. But I'll be honest with you, I've never heard of this. But it's a grave concern, hands down."

Despite this massive debt not appearing in any recovery plan, the Mayor's office said this: "The Mayor and Act 47 call for addressing this situation with future retirements which gets to the re-negotiation of contracts pertaining to health care costs moving forward. Both the Mayor and the receiver will be addressing this situation in the financial recovery plan." — Bob Philbin

Papst Reporter Outcue:
So now, let's take a look at Harrisburg's financial picture. The city owes $184 million in OPEBs. $310 million of incinerator debt, $70 million of mandated sewage upgrades, possible tens of millions from Strawberry Square. That's about $600 million in debt in a city that only makes about $50 million in annual revenue, and *that's* used for operating costs. Question is, who is going to pay for all of this? Harrisburg simply can't.
END SCRIPT

By City Council's meeting on October 11, the city's future was well beyond uncertain. Council lacked the expertise to devise its own recovery plan and it refused to approve any other. Thus, on this date in 2011, Harrisburg became the first capital city in America to file for Chapter 9 protection under the bankruptcy law.

Capital cities are supposed to be recession proof, especially in a state like PA that has nearly 13 million residents sending all their tax dollars, fees and registrations there. This isn't supposed to happen. After Council hired its bankruptcy attorney, the responses were many and varied.

Council member Susan Brown Wilson (voted yes): "I know there will be a lot of backlash because of this. But you know what, if it's about making sure the people of Harrisburg get their justification and their day in court, then I say let's do it."

Council Member Brad Koplinski (voted yes): "We know this isn't a popular thing to do. We understand that, but we truly believe this is the right thing to do. I believe this is the only thing that will work."

Council Member Patti Kim (voted no, then ran for State Assembly and won): "Those attorneys from our creditors are going to sue us out the wazzoo before we get into bankruptcy court. That is not a good plan for residents." (She was near tears.)

Mayor Linda Thompson: "We have a plan on the table. It's not a perfect plan but nothing is perfect, quite frankly —other than God and my savior Jesus Christ."

Republican Governor Tom Corbett: "I remain a strong proponent for municipal governments tackling their own problems and coming together to develop a fiscal recovery plan when necessary. But when that fails to happen, the state has to take action."

And the state did take action. In his 2011 budget, Governor Corbett—in anticipation of a recalcitrant City Council—signed a measure prohibiting Harrisburg from filing for bankruptcy—a tool city leaders hoped to use as leverage against the bondholders. The state also passed a bill stopping Harrisburg from passing a commuter tax. Philadelphia was allowed to impose commuter taxes when it needed extra cash. So did about a dozen other municipalities. But state politicians don't commute to those cities. They commute to Harrisburg. God forbid, they raise their own taxes.

But Harrisburg's forbiddance of a commuter tax holds even greater significance than the obvious. The possibility of a commuter tax was one of the reasons Harrisburg requested Act 47 status. By the state stripping away that potential revenue, it essentially changed the rules in the middle of the game. If there was ever evidence that state politicians loathed their capital city, this was it. From this point forward, the state was not seen as Harrisburg's ally, but rather its foe.

Making all this even more interesting was the man Council hired as its bankruptcy attorney. In Mark Schwartz's many decades of lawyering, he had developed a reputation as a Jewish pit-bull. With Einstein hair, tortoise-shell glasses, and 70s suits, he garnered plenty of attention. Schwartz had grown up in Harrisburg and worked the legislative floor as a teenager. He was trained as a bond attorney, later became an investment banker and finished his professional career as a whistleblowing attorney. He knew Stephen Reed. He knew the accounting tricks Reed used. He even assisted Reed along the way with certain bond structuring. Following Schwartz's appointment as bankruptcy attorney, he afforded me the exclusive first television interview. True to form, he held nothing back.

Anchor Intro:

We begin with a CBS 21 exclusive on the Capital City in Crisis. The man who Harrisburg City Council hired to lead the capital into bankruptcy is speaking out in his first one-on-one television interview. CBS 21's Chris Papst is live with the Dauphin County Mobile Newsroom in Harrisburg and Chris, many feel this attorney doesn't have a case and is fighting a losing battle. Why is he doing this?

Papst Intro from City Overlook:

Because he thinks what is happening to Harrisburg isn't right. Plus, he also wants to make a statement. When Mark Schwartz first saw what Harrisburg was going through, he felt this was the perfect case to match his experience. He's worked on Capitol Hill; he's been a bond attorney, and an investment banker. And he's using all that knowledge to not only challenge the Governor and the Legislature on bankruptcy, but on how things work.

Package Report:

Mark Schwartz: Harrisburg Bankruptcy Attorney

"You know Harrisburg, there but for the grace of God goes the state of Pennsylvania and every other municipality in Pennsylvania."

Harrisburg City Council bankruptcy attorney Mark Swchartz knows the stakes are high. And he also knows what's coming.

Mark Schwartz: Harrisburg Bankruptcy Attorney

"It's a fight. I mean, it's a fight."

So he's taking the first swings. In a recently published op-ed Schwartz went after Governor Corbett, questioning his intentions.

Mark Schwartz: Harrisburg Bankruptcy Attorney

"There's something absolutely perverse about a Governor who on one day basically gives a check of $11.5 million to a healthy investment bank in Philadelphia and the next day signs takeover legislation saying it's really important for municipalities to be self-reliant."

That money went to the firm Janney Montgomery Scott. And Schwartz wants to know why an investment firm can get millions from the state while Harrisburg gets taken over.

Mark Schwartz: Harrisburg Bankruptcy Attorney

"This is just a mockery."

Schwartz also questions the Legislature's intentions behind municipal tax structure. By not letting cities like Harrisburg have a sales tax, Schwartz says the state is causing them to fail.

Mark Schwartz: Harrisburg Bankruptcy Attorney

"I don't understand why what's good for Pittsburgh in the form of an extra sales tax, or what is good for Philadelphia is not also good for Harrisburg. What this speaks to is the failure of the Governor and the general assembly to address local tax reform."

Papst Reporter Outcue:

And of course, Schwartz wants all that to change. And this situation gives him the platform to talk about it.
END SCRIPT

The reputation Schwartz had built for himself was one of aggression. His tactics in the courtroom were often chastised by judges and the media. He seemed to thrive while on the attack with insinuations and assumptions that make the room uncomfortable and his targets squirm. The mere mention of his name seemed to draw only adoration or scorn—not much in between.

Here is the second story I did on him.

Anchor Intro:

We begin with a CBS 21 exclusive on the Capital City in Crisis. The man who Harrisburg City Council hired to lead the capital into bankruptcy is speaking out in his first one-on-one television interview. CBS 21's Chris Papst is live with the Dauphin County Mobile Newsroom in Harrisburg and Chris, yesterday you talked with Mark Schwartz about why he took on this case and today you hit the big topic, bankruptcy.

Papst Intro from City Island:

It's pretty rare that attorneys openly talk to the media about cases while they're in court. But, as you are about to see Mark Schwartz has his plan drawn out as to why Harrisburg's bankruptcy was legal and why the state's attempt to stop it, is unconstitutional. And he has no reservations; he's going at the Governor and the Legislature.

Package Report:

Mark Schwartz: Harrisburg Bankruptcy Attorney

"Yeah, I'd say historic. It's historic. But, it's not like it's something that's impossible."

In fact, Harrisburg City Council bankruptcy attorney Mark Schwartz believes it's the exact opposite; his winning in court is entirely possible. And the strategy is simple.

Mark Schwartz: Harrisburg Bankruptcy Attorney

"I'll go through the cases. I'll go through the Pennsylvania Constitution. I'll go through applicable statutes."

What's at issue is the state law passed earlier this year that prohibits Harrisburg from filing for bankruptcy. Even though it received overwhelming bi-partisan support from both Houses of the Legislature and was enthusiastically signed by Governor Corbett, Schwartz says that bill is unconstitutional for two reasons. First, the PA Constitution prohibits *specific* legislation. And even though the bill was written to apply to all third class cities, Schwartz challenges the intent.

Mark Schwartz: Harrisburg Bankruptcy Attorney

"It said no Third Class CITY that is DISTRESSED. That's like putting a bull's eye on your forehead. Who else could that be?"

Schwartz also says the bill didn't meet general standards of legislation and is historically problematic.

Mark Schwartz: Harrisburg Bankruptcy Attorney

"The political process has been a failure."

According to Mayor Thompson, what is problematic is the filing itself. Her spokesman tells CBS 21 that "Schwartz was not hired legally by City Council. The Mayor has filed an objection in court because Council violated city ordinance, they can't hire someone to represent the city."

Schwartz disagrees saying Act 47 changed that, allowing Council to hire a lawyer.

Papst Reporter Outcue:

We did reach out to the Governor's office, Senator Piccola, Representative Grell, and numerous City Council members for comment. The only person who we could get to respond to Schwartz was the Mayor's spokesman.

END SCRIPT

As lawyers, bond attorneys, Council members, the Governor and Mayor fought over who would control Harrisburg, apparently Mother Nature felt left out. It was also in 2011 that she exploited its weakness. Days of heavy rain in early September sent the Susquehanna River and surrounding waterways to historic levels.

Significant flooding of rivers and creeks is an odd thing. Water levels do not crest until days after the rain has moved out. Oftentimes, under a bright sun, residents prepare for the worst by stacking sandbags and moving their belonging upstairs. Science has progressed to where time lines and water levels can be accurately calculated days in advance. So in other words, we know how bad it's going to get. And what happened in September of 2011, following Tropical Storm Lee, was bad.

The Susquehanna River is the 16th largest river system in the nation. With a width of half a mile, floods are not common. River flow is measured in cubic feet per second, or CFS. The Susquehanna averages about 34,000. But after Lee dropped upward of 10 inches, the Susquehanna rose to channel nearly 18 times that amount. At its peak, it was sending 590,000 cubic feet of water per second towards the Chesapeake Bay. For the Susquehanna, this was the fifth worst flood in recorded history. But nearby creeks and streams, such as the Swatara, broke all-time records.

Roller coaster rails at Hershey Park were underwater. Large animals trapped in lower areas of the zoo were euthanized before they drowned. Schools, parks, campgrounds and highways were closed. Those schools that didn't close, or evacuate on time, were forced to harbor the students. Thousands of homes and businesses lost power. City Island was a pool, as was the playing field of the Senators baseball stadium. And I was in my knee waders covering it.

Standing at the edge of rising water is about as ominous an experience as I've ever had. The only thing I can compare it to is watching the approaching clouds of a category five hurricane—another experience I'm blessed to have. At one point, I remember placing my toes at the water's edge. The river had already breached its banks and was creeping onto Front Street. Within minutes, the water had reached my heels and was working its way over the crest of my boots.

Floodwaters appear alive. Like a wild animal, its actions are predictable, yet nearly impossible to contain.

But unlike other natural disasters, the chaos arrives slowly and strikes with no intensity. People scramble for hours or days to secure their homes and prepare belongings—only to be left waiting and hoping.

With miles of streets and hundreds of homes partially or fully underwater, Harrisburg was placed under a state of emergency. Mother Nature had somehow achieved what seemed impossible; she further burdened the spirits of an exhausted and broken people.

Weeks later, with much of Harrisburg floating in the Atlantic Ocean, the repairs began. Most homeowners and businesses had flood insurance. But this was not the case in 1972 when the city experienced the worst natural disaster in its history. And much like the 2011 storm, Mother Nature picked the worst possible time to strike.

It was in 1972 that Hurricane Agnes raised the Susquehanna River to its highest level since records began in 1786. Every second, 1,000,000 cubic feet of water rushed south.

Agnes proved significant for a number of reasons. First, it produced an unlikely and unsung hero in Stephen Reed. At age 22, he participated and managed the rescue. He saved scores of people and property. River Rescue made him a hero and a popular public figure.

The second significant aspect of Agnes was that it finished off a city that was wobbling from multiple blows. Plus, unlike natural disasters of today, the Federal government was less likely to offer assistance in the 70s. Six thousand houses did not have flood insurance. The then Mayor of Harrisburg said the flooding had an impact of "3,000 to 5,000 fires." More than 600 small businesses were destroyed, 12,000 sustained damage (Beers). Four hundred national guardsmen were called in to stop people from boating up and down the streets. Agnes didn't arrive raining hell. She arrived with little interest. But when she reversed directions and dropped 13 inches on the region, she showed that weather is never to be underestimated. The flood also knocked out the water filtration plant. Yet another achievement of the City Beautiful Movement was lost.

The Mayor at the time delivered a rousing address by claiming, "[the city] suffered its greatest disaster in history and it survived. A weak, wobbly, dying city could not have done that" (Beers). How inspiring.

After the flood, Harrisburg looked even less attractive to residents and businesses. With the advent of FEMA in 1978 and now with a more direct Federal focus on disaster relief, the flood of 2011 was not nearly as significant. But, it did serve to highlight the dangers of a mis-run and unorganized government.

2011 was indeed a terrible year, during which you may have wondered the whereabouts of Stephen Reed? And that's a good question.

It's also worth mentioning that a few days after Mayor Thompson locked me out of that press conference, I talked to a photographer who was inside. He said the microphone on his camera recorded the sound of me knocking. And he said we could have it. I immediately went to my news director. We had saved the recording from that night, including the sound with the Communications Director who said he could not hear me knocking.

"We caught the Mayor's office in a lie," I explained to my news director. "I can have the story ready by tomorrow."

Indeed, I did have everything I needed for a great story, except an interested news director. He refused to run it.

11: BOW TO THE STATE

OR HARRISBURG, 2012 BEGAN in much the same fashion as 2011 ended. The city was still broke, (if anything, it was more broke), its debtors and bills were still not being paid, City Council and the Mayor were still not talking and it still had no recovery plan. But none of that really mattered anymore, because by the time residents rang in the New Year, the state had already taken over. Harrisburg no longer controlled its own destiny.

"Ladies and gentleman," Mayor Thompson declared in her presser (press conference) following the takeover, "the Governor is now going to take the city. It's over. It's over. It's over. We have no idea what our future looks like now." As if she had any idea what it looked like before.

In all fairness, before the takeover, the state did give her and Council a fourth chance to approve a recovery plan. They failed.

"This is just awful, simply awful, basically—no doubt about it."

"Yeah," I lamented as I sped down Interstate 81 on the way to work.

"What's wrong?" By this point, we had developed enough of a professional relationship to where he knew something was bothering me.

"I don't know, man," I replied. "I'm just getting tired of covering this shit show. I'm sort of over it."

"What do you mean?" His loud coughs were even more painful as they shrieked through my car's speakers. "What are you over?"

"All this ridiculous nonsense. It's been a year-and-a-half, and the city just keeps getting worse," I explained. "Everyone in charge is either incompetent, crooked, or has some political agenda."

"Oh, yeah."

"I'm tired of covering murders, sinkholes, blight, collapsed buildings and sleazy lawyers. I don't want to talk to another crying mother or disingenuous politician. It's every day, man. And the assholes that caused this mess refuse to talk to anyone and just want their millions. And you know what? They'll probably get it. And they *knew* the city could never pay back all that money. Meanwhile, the city and its people are suffering—*because* of them—and they don't give a shit. It's maddening." I had to stop for a breath.

"Why should they be owed anything? They agreed to those loans knowing the city was a house of cards. They took that risk. What about their responsibility? The whole damn thing is just draining." I would have referred to him by his name, but I still didn't know it. "I want it to be over. I can't believe I'm about to say this, but isn't there a surfing squirrel somewhere I can report on?"

He laughed. "I understand. But you can't stop now." His voice rose with a rare passion. "The media is the only *real* check and balance we have. Politicians don't monitor each other. They're mostly lawyers protecting each other's power. Harrisburg is where it is because the media, for years, wasn't doing its job, basically—no doubt about it. Had someone been reporting on Reed honestly, the city wouldn't be in this position because people would have known."

"Maybe."

"Not maybe," he softened. "Absolutely."

The few seconds of silence following, allowed me to realize he was indeed right.

"How are the stories coming?" His tone normalized. "Do you need anything else from us?"

"No," I sighed. "I have everything I need. I'm just finalizing some things. We're focusing on Reed with the bank accounts and how he siphoned cash for his pet projects. More people were willing to talk than I thought. We have good stuff."

"Good," he replied. "I'll be in touch next week. Just make sure you give me the air dates in advance. There's plenty of people that want to see these reports. I need time to alert them."

"I will."

"Hang in there, Chris."

When the line deadened, the news came alive. Their top story—an update to the lawsuit Mayor Thompson filed against the City Controller, Dan Miller. The same Controller she likened a "homosexual, evil little man."

She was suing to force the Controller to sign off on her plan to sell a collection of Wild West Artifacts Mayor Reed had purchased while in office. This suit was one amongst many and got relatively little attention. The others were far more substantial.

Soon after City Council stood up to the state and financial world by hiring a bankruptcy attorney, a federal court swiftly rejected the filing. The judge, in part, feared if Harrisburg were allowed to go bankrupt, 20 other municipalities in the state would follow. This prompted an enraged Mark Schwartz to disparage the judge for lacking a "fundamental understanding of statutory interpretation." Notwithstanding the legal rationale, the terrifying aspect of her ruling may lay in its accuracy. But to what extent is that rationale prudent? Without bankruptcy, how can a failing city survive any more than a struggling company or individual?

Prior to this judge's ruling, every elected member of Harrisburg's government, except for Mayor Thompson, favored bankruptcy. The Controller, Treasurer (who in mid-2104 was charged with felony theft for stealing thousands from a Democrat organization and a non-profit) and a majority of Council had formed a strong case to seek Chapter 9 protection. But without the Mayor's support, the judge questioned the filing's legitimacy.

Thompson felt bankruptcy was embarrassing and a ploy to make her look bad. The agitated Mayor wailed in paranoia, "I am unapologetic in saying the Controller has his hands in this. He announced he's running for mayor. Brad Koplinski (outspoken Council member) has been the quiet one. We know he is going to try to run for mayor, as well (which he didn't). They want to be able to blame bankruptcy filing on me. They want to blame the state takeover on me. I don't have time to deal with that nonsense. I have to stay focused. I am the mayor right now and I plan on continue governing."

City Controller Dan Miller responded, "Because it's so inevitable, when you look at these numbers, there's really one thing that is going to happen. Is the state going to force us to sell and lease assets prior to going to bankruptcy, or are we going to be able to go into bankruptcy and protect those assets?"

Either way, the end of that court battle led directly to another. Following the federal judge's bankruptcy ruling, a civil rights suit was filed challenging the constitutionality of the state takeover.

This is what I reported when the suit was filed:

"This federal suit was filed by three residents of Harrisburg: Nevin Midlin, a former candidate for mayor; Eric Jenkins, a union leader; and Reverend Earl Harris of St. Paul Baptist Church. They are asking a judge to throw out the bill that allowed the state takeover of the city. The suit names Governor Corbett and the man he nominated to be the receiver, David Unkovic. In the suit, it says the bill is unconstitutional because it violates the rights of due process and equal protection. The suit also says the bill violates the state's constitution because it suspends representative democracy in the city."

All the challenges to the takeover and prohibition against bankruptcy ultimately failed, too. Much to the joy of the Mayor, who proclaimed upon the conclusion of the last suit: "Truly, I can attest that it is a day to give thanks."

"The citizens of Harrisburg don't deserve what they are going to get," replied a somber, almost ominous, Schwartz. "But the Mayor does, and her bones are going to be absolutely picked by this receiver."

I found it odd, the degree to which the American and international medias cared about Harrisburg's plight. Following the initial bankruptcy filing, the global press swarmed. They correctly understood the significance of that moment. But then it died off. Some large media, such as Reuters and the Bond Buyer, continued to follow the story, but most didn't. I get it. What was happening in the Keystone State was not sexy. But perhaps that's one of the reasons the American media has lost such credibility with the people—they prefer sexy over relevant.

In reality, the result of Harrisburg's crisis affected millions. And while this was not the topic of conversation at most Commonwealth and American dinner tables, it was being watched very closely. Cash-strapped municipalities—and there are plenty—across the fruited plain were interested, because if Harrisburg ultimately filed for bankruptcy and was able to rewrite its debt contracts, other municipalities would surely follow. The judge was right. But they wouldn't just follow in Pennsylvania. They would follow across the United States. The run on the municipal bond market could be disastrous. If the housing bubble bust was bad, what would the muni-bond bubble bust look like?

Plus, you'd think more people would care simply due to the amount of money wasted on "saving" Harrisburg. Lawyers and consultants made millions, which the city desperately needed.

Anyway, soon after Governor Corbett signed the takeover legislation hastily drafted by the Legislature, he nominated Philadelphia bond attorney, David Unkovic, as receiver.

Tall and thin, with a friendly face, Unkovic aesthetically appealed to everyone. He was soft in voice, and despite his Harvard Law School education and subsequent pedigree, he spoke in a manner of zero disdain. He appeared a commoner.

"My goal is to get the best plan we can and to involve everybody in the process along the way," he said in his first press conference. "I look forward to working closely with the Mayor. She is the chief elected official of the city elected by the residents. I respect that and I respect her as a public official." He had to say that.

Unkovic knew from the beginning he not only needed to understand the financial status of the city, he also had to win over its residents, which may have been his greatest challenge. This is a city that's three-quarters minority with a more lopsided minority elected leadership. Now, an old white guy with gray hair (the Governor), appointed an equally as old white guy with gray hair (the receiver) to run Pennsylvania's capital city. And this old white guy usurped the power of a democratically elected minority government. The optics were terrible and Unkovic knew it.

The Philadelphia resident had 32-years of experience in public finance, mostly as a bond attorney. "I am going to pursue this with great determination to come up with the best possible plan for the city. We'll push the process as fast as we can. I'd like the people of the city to know this problem is solvable." He delivered all his lines with zero uncertainty. It was refreshing.

The only aspect of his resume that prevented him from being the perfect candidate was his apparent conflicts of interest. During his storied career, he had worked for at least three firms that had direct connections to city creditors, which stood to make or lose a lot of money in this process. When this was discovered, you can imagine the city's reaction.

The biggest complaints from those who opposed the ACT 47 plans was that there was not enough shared pain —there was not a "global solution." Meaning: all the parties involved in the incinerator and debt debacle should be involved in the sacrificial fix. Now, many feared the man nominated to solve the problem had a direct interest in making sure Wall Street got paid in full—since he used to work there.

I asked Unkovic if this apparent conflict of interest should worry city residents.

"I have no contact with those firms anymore and I am going to do what is in the best interest of the city in this situation," he told me. "The municipal bond industry in Pennsylvania is small. Anybody who has been in the industry for 32 years is going to know just about everybody else who's in that industry."

Ok, I thought. That makes sense.

Given the degree of public outcry over Unkovic's past employers, I sought out Harrisburg state Representative, Democrat Ron Buxton. He represented the city. I was curious as to his thoughts. I did not expect him to say this, "I discussed that [conflicts of interest] with [Unkovic] two weeks ago and said you will be judged critically in Harrisburg with some of the ties you've had in the past. And I said the only way that you can prove to the citizens of Harrisburg that this is not going to be a problem in negotiations is to be able to show you are really representing them and doing a job for the citizens of Harrisburg and not doing anything special for those stakeholders."

Unkovic must have taken those words to heart. Before his nomination was approved, he ran the public relations gauntlet, which he was under no obligation to do. He conducted town hall meetings to talk to residents and answer their questions. He walked the streets to shake hands and attended city functions. All the while, holding meetings with city creditors and unions to secure concessions.

"I'm not at liberty to talk right now in detail about what is going on in negotiations," Unkovic would say in a very sincere way. This was a question he would often get from residents. "But I am talking with people and looking forward to continuing to talk with them to come up with a plan that is going to work for the city."

I watched closely as he interacted with the people. I examined his body language, his eye contact, his expressions. I listened intently to his words. I was trying hard to find something not to like. The city had been screwed so hard for so long, I found it difficult to believe Harrisburg had finally landed a winner. But after observing him for a few weeks, I was truly impressed. At first, my skepticism was extremely high. But he won me over. I personally believed he was the right person for the job. With him in power, for the first time, I honestly felt Harrisburg had a fighting chance.

And I wasn't the only skeptic he won over. At first, City Council and other city officials thwarted his nomination citing the conflicts of interest. But they too soon came to admire and believe in him—though they still favored bankruptcy.

Mayor Thompson seemed to love him from the start. She argued his conflicts weren't a big concern because he wouldn't directly profit. Although, at this point, her relationship with Council was so chaotic that if Council did one thing she automatically did the other—and visa-versa. Her immediate support of Unkovic was viewed as a result of Council's opposition.

According to the recently passed legislation, a Commonwealth Court judge had the ultimate task of approving or denying the receiver's nomination. Which was basically a rubber stamp. City Council and the Mayor had no role in the process. The state wouldn't dare empower them with further responsibility. Thus, they had been rendered utterly insignificant. The people's elected officials were truly stripped of their power to determine the city's future. It was now up to judges and unelected nominees.

So, when it came time for the receiver's public hearing before Commonwealth Court, Council's attorney Mark Schwartz was ready to pounce. He had thoroughly prepared his arguments and showed up in court ready to fight. In a room full of cozy seriousness, he was the lone antagonist. He saw Unkovic's nomination as a sham that must be exposed. But, in a shocking move, the Judge dismissed Schwartz from the courtroom before he even had time to organize his documents.

"I'm being dismissed?" He wickedly snapped, mouth and eyes opened wide.

When the hearing began, Unkovic was the only person who took the stand. The courtroom was largely occupied with reporters and lawyers. A pissed off Schwartz sat taut in the front row, scowling at the judge. With Schwartz forbidden to cross-examine Unkovic, he was only questioned by known supporters.

I sat in the courtroom that day watching this dog and pony show questioning its necessity. The fix was clearly in. There wasn't a court in the state that would have rejected his nomination. And the legislators that wrote the bill knew that. So, why was our time being wasted? The people who knew the city and its people best, Council and the Mayor, weren't even at the hearing. They knew it for what it really was.

After court adjourned, Schwartz opined, "I was appointed by Council to represent them. I would not have asked the softball questions that were asked." He had yet to calm down. "It's politics that get people like [Unkovic] appointed to his current job and to bond Council positions. OK? This isn't all happenstance."

When Unkovic emerged from the courtroom, he too addressed the media. Though, his voice lacked Schwartz's zeal. "From the time I was nominated by the Governor to now I have been reaching out, talking to people who are involved and interested in the city. I'm learning as much as I can and I do want to come up with the best possible solution after getting as much information as possible." His delivery made you want to believe.

"I don't see how he can serve and frankly he should have taken himself out of it," demanded Schwartz. His voice was high with incredulity. "Government is not supposed to just adhere to whether there's an *actual* conflict of interest, it is supposed to adhere to whether there is the *appearance* of a conflict of interest. This is a farce. The Governor might as well pick someone who made a lot of money on the Harrisburg incinerator bond issue."

Perhaps the only real positive so far of the takeover and the receiver's nomination is that—after all this—if Harrisburg went down, Governor Tom Corbett went down with it. An inconvenience that did help residents sleep a little better.

Besides the takeover and the appointment of the receiver, there is one other thing that made 2012 different from 2011 in Harrisburg. The city didn't have a budget. In November, the Mayor did draft a budget, but Council claimed it wasn't balanced and rewrote it. They cut $1.2 million and 12 city positions—one of which was Director of Communications. In other words, the Mayor's spokesman. Council argued that similarly sized cities in PA didn't have one, so why should Harrisburg? Hence, yet another fight emerged.

I pressed one of the original "gang of four" members about the cut, I was told, "Would you rather have a spokesman or would you rather have a fireman? These are the choices that we have to make. We can't keep kicking this can down the road. We have to make the tough choices."

When Council sent the budget back to the Mayor, she promptly held a press conference and called Council "reckless" and "irresponsible." She chastised the city's legislative branch for creating an "illegal" budget that violated city mandates.

"I cannot allow the dysfunction of City Council to permeate city government," she shrieked in front of the camera. "We cannot allow that dysfunction to disrupt the health, safety and welfare of our city and our visitors." She went on to say not having a Communications Director put "residents at risk" since no one was left to speak for the city.

So, Thompson vetoed the budget and called Council a bunch of "cowards" with their "smokes and mirrors (sic)". The "cowards" then voted 6-1 to override her veto and fired her spokesman. This too, was another first in the city. Never before had a budget bounced back and forth so many times. It was now weeks into the new year, and still no budget. Meanwhile, the suburbs just kept slowly shaking their heads in disappointment. But in reality, none of this mattered. The receiver's pending plan would trump it all, anyway.

This rift only served to further bolster the state's position in the takeover. The public hatred between the city's legislative and executive branches caused nothing to get done.

"I just wish City Council and the Mayor had a new year's resolution to just stop bashing each other," declared a mournful Council member, Patty Kim. Kim was perhaps the least important of all the Council members. Her passivity allowed for her complete overshadowing by her colleagues. She lacked any semblance of conviction or leadership. Her vision for the city was unclear as she floated in the breeze of indecision. But in the process, she didn't make as many enemies and became the only member of that Council to achieve higher office as a state Representative. So goes politics.

It was also during this time that Harrisburg quit paying its General Obligation Debt, or GO debt. This was yet another historical "first" for the capital. Basically, GO debt is the mortgage of a city. This is debt the city uses to buy police cars or trash trucks. The debt is paid twice annually, once early in the year and again in the fall. The payments that were skipped were for $2.7 million and $2.5 million. They were both bonds from 1997. Receiver Unkovic said this was not an easy decision, but it was necessary. The city simply did not have the money to pay its firemen and policemen and this debt.

"I think the city has worked hard not to default on the General Obligation Debt until now. But when you look at the cash flow for the city this year, I think it's important we continue to provide vital and necessary services to the city including police, fire, water and so forth," said Unkovic.

For those who favored bankruptcy, this move further demonstrated how bankrupt the city really was. In reality, had a business or household not had the money for this equivalent GO debt, it would surely trigger a Chapter 13, Chapter 11 or Chapter 7 filing.

"This just raises the seriousness of our financial situation to a whole new level. It signals that we are not only defaulting on guaranteed debt, we're defaulting to basically all of our creditors. So now we're going to be sued or pursued by everyone," stated the "homosexual, evil little" city Controller.

Meanwhile, as all this chaos was happening, criminals saw opportunity in a vulnerable city and took advantage of it. With no budget, money or future in sight, crime spiked.

When I wasn't watching Council yell at each other, listening to the Mayor blame her troubles on someone else or sitting in some Commonwealth Court at another rubber stamp proceeding, I was covering this drastic increase in crime.

In the nicer sections of the city, to combat the misconduct, residents fought simply for working streetlights. If you were to walk around much of Harrisburg at night, the one thing you're sure to notice is that it's hard to see. Just along the waterfront from north to south, I once counted dozens of burnt out lights. From the bridges leading into the city, to outside the Capitol, to right across the street from the Governor's Residence, when the sun goes down over Harrisburg, many places stay dark.

"It's a tedious task hampered by limited dollars," said the city Communications Director, whose job was now just as uncertain as the city's future. "It's a matter of priority. Is that light as important on the walking bridge as it is on Front Street or Mid Town?"

City residents were tired of excuses and even more tired of being victims. "Right now we are dealing with a bad crime problem and in some of our neighborhoods I think lighting would help the situation," one resident told me when I did this story. "Yeah, I think there's a solution. Since the city is broke right now I think a community effort would be in order."

And that community effort did happen. After my story aired, an anonymous person donated $10,000 to repair all the lights on the walking bridge from City Island to the mainland. It was a great effort, but it was all aesthetic. This bridge was primarily what motorists saw at night from the highways. It did little to calm the residents' fear of criminals. Although, it made the city look less broke.

In March of 2012, Harrisburg set another city record when it was ranked the 20th most dangerous city in America by a crime reporting agency. With 15 violent crimes per 1,000 residents, Harrisburg was five times more dangerous than Philly. Before winter ended, four people had already been murdered. Muggings were rampant. The evidence of this report was all around. Yet, Mayor Thompson disputed the study saying violent crimes were half of what they used to be. But, she did admit robberies have doubled. Then, she asked for $500,000 from the county to hire more policemen.

"We're not going to be fearful of the perpetrator," she told the media. For this presser, I was not locked out. "We want it to be reversed. We want the perpetrator to be afraid of us. Because we're not going to let no one take over our city (except the state). Would I like to be on any list at all? Absolutely not. But crime is inevitable. And the thing is to keep our hands on top of it."

These words came at about the time a cab driver was shot in the head during a robbery.

Harrisburg was so impotent, midtown area residents were forced to form their own "Improvement District."

"I think it's very important for us to get together and throw more eyes out there because we can keep them away," one resident told me.

The Midtown Improvement District was designed to collect fees from property owners to hire off-duty Harrisburg Police officers to patrol. The average resident would pay $60 a year. Businesses would pay more. The group's founder, Eric Papenfuse, a local bookstore owner, says they could hire as many as eight officers a night.

"I think so many people have been affected by crime that they really feel now is the time to do something about it," said Papenfuse.

"I think it's great when people don't just depend on a higher authority or government to take care of them," one group member said.

Meanwhile, on the other side of the city, The Allison Hill neighborhood which has much less money also tried to find a solution. But they couldn't afford to hire off-duty cops—nor would they want to.

"Now-a-days, the younger people like 13 and 14, they decide they can hold guns. But when we were that age we were scared of guns," one resident spoke up and said at their emergency meeting.

This meeting was very different than the one in midtown. Aside from the difference in wealth, those in the midtown area were fighting back against robberies, vandalism and purse snatching. Those in Allison Hill were battling murders, shootings and stabbings. Here, young people and adults just talked about their options to stop the violence—violence that in 2009 took the life of Tracy Davis' 20-year-old son.

"The violence in this city is getting ridiculous," said Davis in near tears. "Too many mothers are losing their children."

Davis' son was shot and killed in his own home.

"I've attended five memorials since my son was killed for other children that have been gunned down in the streets of Harrisburg. And it's sad."

A man named Shawn Vaughan told me he has seen the city's youth drastically change in just the last few years. He said they've become emboldened and less afraid.

"We are scared of them because we have an understanding that they kill," he said. "Tonight I'm trying to get a little bit of understanding of how the people feel. And let them know how I feel. Hopefully we can build something from there."

While sitting in a chair watching the discussion, I saw something in an older lady's purse.

I lightly tapped her on the shoulder. "What did you bring with you tonight?"

"I got the spray," she told me uncertain of its true effectiveness. "Why? I can't leave home without it. We are not safe anymore. We're seniors, we don't stand a chance. I can't even walk the neighborhood, anymore. It's very, very scary."

This happened to be a meeting Mayor Thompson attended. She did little to comfort the group by saying this: "This is our neighborhood and you are not going to come up in here and act like you are a wild, wild west individual." Unfortunately, they already were.

As for me, all this culminated in the following story from March 29. Use your imagination and try to picture this scene as described. It was crazy.

Anchor Intro:

Intense moments this evening on Derry Street in Harrisburg as a nine-year-old girl is run over by a pick-up truck and then minutes later a high speed pursuit on that same road ends in a horrific crash that sends two people to the hospital on stretchers. CBS 21's Chris Papst is live with the Dauphin County Mobile Newsroom in Harrisburg; and Chris you were involved in all of this...?

Papst Reporter Intro from Scene where car wrapped around telephone pole:

Yes, I was. We originally came here to cover that 9-year-old girl you mentioned that was hit by the truck. Then all of sudden around 6:45 police on the scene started screaming for everyone to get back and leave the street and sidewalk. They hollered that a high-speed pursuit was coming down Derry Street right where we were. But as you can see, it never made it to us. (I knelt down to show debris from the wreck one block from where the girl was run over).

Package Report:

The scene was chaotic... (People fleeing the street as a high-speed police chase approaches down the hill.)

...and dramatic. (Up close shot of rescue crews cutting open a car to rescue unconscious survivors after crash. Once the roof came off, crews toss out of the car a large birthday cake, which splatters on the ground. Onlookers release a collective gasp.)

At about 6:45, the driver of this stolen car was leading Swatara Police on a high-speed chase down Derry Street in Harrisburg. When the driver got to this block, he saw the road was blocked by police due to a nine-year-old who was hit by a truck a short while before. The driver tried to quickly turn and smashed (t-boned) this Toyota into a telephone pole (with the three people in the Toyota severely injured). The two men inside the green car ran. One was captured minutes later (crowd cheers as police handcuff him) as rescue crews rushed to save the lives of the people he just hit. (Shots of crews using jaws-of-life on victim's car.)

Unique Davis: First Responder

"I seen the son yelling and screaming. He was stuck in the car. So I ran over there and got the son out."

Unique Davis watched the crash happen from a stop sign on the opposite side of the street. She was forced to get involved.

Unique Davis: First Responder

"Was it pretty scary? Yeah it was. I literally couldn't put my car in park fast enough to get that little boy out the car. My only concern was getting that little boy out of the car."

The little boy turned out to be fine. Unfortunately, the little girl who once wore this jacket (jacket lying on street) just two blocks away was not so lucky. After buying snacks at this convenience store, the girl ran into the street towards this playground and was hit by this oncoming pick-up truck. Her candy went everywhere. Shana Terry rushed to her aid.

Shana Terry: First Responder

"She was conscious. She was going in and out. I knelt down and held her head and told her it was going to be OK."

Terry said the young girl was bleeding from her nose, mouth and ears. She held her in her arms until help arrived.

Shana Terry: First Responder

"She wasn't responding at all. Her eyes were rolled in the back of her head. It looked like she was about to die."

Papst Outcue:
And the hospital has confirmed the young girl has died.
END SCRIPT

During this disastrous time, Mayor Thompson desperately wanted to look relevant and in control. Her own desire for a receiver stripped her of her mayoral responsibility. So she embarked on a crusade to collect delinquent loans. In all, the city was owed $850,000 that apparently had just been forgotten.

When Thompson released the list, I tracked down some of the businesses.

"I spoke with people in the city," said the owner of an auto shop in the midtown area. "We are going to set up a meeting and we are going to work this out."

Troy Peiffer owns Peiffer Auto Repair. A few years prior when things got tough he took a loan from the city. And when things got tougher he couldn't make the payments. He owed $22,500.

"I want to work this out with the city," he told me. "I want the city to grow. I want my business to grow. I want to be here for a long time."

But many of the businesses that received loans from Harrisburg were no longer in business. The owner of Jersey City Clothing got $11,000 and then shut his doors.

Then there's a man named David Dodd. Even though people were home when I paid him a visit, no one answered. He owed the city a whopping $308,000. His neighbors told me the FBI had also recently wanted to ask him some questions. A few years later, he was sentenced to 87 months in federal prison for fraud involving the construction of a city complex. I wonder who loaned him that $308,000 he never paid back. Any guesses?

Anyway, to further increase city revenues and clean up a bit, Thompson next launched an aggressive campaign to cite landowners for improper land management. The city quickly issued more than 200 citations for property violations, which included uncut vegetation. On one particular block, the city issued about half a dozen citations.

Given this block's harsh treatment, I took a drive in search of outspoken landowners. During my journey, one specific property caught my attention. The address was 2549 N. 6th Street and it clearly hadn't been cut in years. The weeds were nearly as tall as I am. Yet, an old couch and a slew of stuffed trash bags were still clearly visible. You can imagine my surprise when I discovered this property hadn't been cited. Though, it made sense when I learned who owned it, The Harrisburg Redevelopment Authority.

"They talk about cleaning up the city because of all the trash and so forth, yet they won't do anything about something of this nature?" said Bill Hooper, a resident who operates a tax business next to the unkempt lot. Hooper ran up to me as I drove down the street looking for a story. "It's a double standard. If you were a citizen, you would be fined for something of this nature. If you are part of Harrisburg or the Harrisburg Redevelopment Authority, then it's OK? It's not OK. It gives the idea that we live like this and we don't."

That day, my story ran. The next day at Mayor Thompson's presser, I tried to get a comment from her. She didn't even let me finish my question.

"I know exactly what you're talking about. I saw your negative little story," she barked. "We have a huge number of vacant lots we contract out for that work. We have put in a very progressive and aggressive work plan for them to get out there."

The next day, after years of neglect, the lot was cut.

The city had certainly been through a lot around this time. But for what happened next, it was not at all prepared.

Anchor Intro:

The uncertain future of Harrisburg just got far more uncertain. The man appointed by Governor Corbett to lead the city out of this financial crisis, David Unkovic, has suddenly and unexpectedly resigned as receiver. He filed the papers today with the Commonwealth Court. CBS 21's Chris Papst joins us live from the Dauphin County Mobile Newsroom in Harrisburg and Chris, what does this mean for the city and its recovery?

Papst Intro from City Island:

It's hard to put into words how much this exactly affects the city because it affects so many things. Harrisburg already doesn't have enough money to operate. Earlier this month, for the first time ever, the city missed a General Obligation Debt payment. And now it has no receiver, it has no leader for the recovery.

Reporter Package:
Brad Koplinski: City Council ("gang of four" member)
"This is a sad day for Harrisburg. Mr. Unkovic was on the right track. He was digging up answers and finding the right solutions. We were all happy to work with him. He was fair and honest with everyone he spoke with."

Most everyone seemed to agree, David Unkovic was doing a great job as the receiver for Pennsylvania's capital city. His resignation surprised everyone, even the man who appointed him.

Kevin Harley: Governor's Press Secretary
"Tom Corbett believes his resignation is both unexpected and unfortunate. We thought he was doing a wonderful job."

But over the past few weeks Unkovic's demeanor has steadily changed in the face of his monumental task of turning around Harrisburg. At first, he was optimistic and jovial. But as time wore on and he learned more about how Harrisburg got into this mess and its chances of getting out, he started to noticeably change. He got more emotional during press conferences and less optimistic. (Drastic pictures of how Unkovic changed over his time as receiver.) It was obvious the stress was getting to him.

Brad Koplinski: City Council
"This is huge. I'm mad. This is a blow that is going to be very difficult to come through because this is going to set the process back months."

Everyone we talked to today expressed that David Unkovic's resignation is a setback for the city in some way—everyone except Mayor Thompson.

In a press conference today, the Mayor said that Unkovic did not work alone and there is a team in place, which includes her, which will follow through with the recovery plan. Before Unkovic resigned, he drew up a very basic plan for recovery that he said would need a lot of work. The Mayor said there are people left who can do that work, such as contract negotiations and determining the value of city assets. She said she will continue to implement the receiver's plan.

Linda Thompson: Harrisburg Mayor

"This is not a setback. It is unfortunate that Mr. Unkovic has resigned. It came at an unexpected time. Of course, we would have preferred him to have not resigned. But the fact of the matter is it's a part of life. And no one died. The city is not shut down. Business is still running. The city is still open and we are moving forward with the recovery plan."

Papst Outcue:

The Governor will now have to find a new person to appoint as receiver and we will have to go through the entire process again of that person being approved. Then, the new receiver will have to be educated on the city. So this entire process, many think, will set the city back months, but it doesn't have months. Harrisburg can't pay its bills now.

Anchor Question:

So what about the plan that the receiver drew up, is that still being implemented?

Papst Answer:

I asked the Governor's Press Secretary that exact question and he didn't seem to have an answer. No one knows what happens now. This has never happened before in the history of not only Pennsylvania, but America. Everything that is happening right now in Harrisburg is unprecedented.

END SCRIPT

It's hard to accurately quantify the significance of Unkovic's resignation. It was yet another devastating blow after a string of devastating blows. If there were one phrase I heard repeated it was, "It can't get any worse." And in this instance it may have truly applied.

In a city where its leaders disagree on most everything, everyone agreed that Unkovic was the right person for the job. He was fair and appeared to have the best interests of the city at heart, which is all anyone could really ask. With him, people were optimistic. Over the past few months, David Unkovic earned respect. Now what?

His departure spawned calls for hearings. Governor Corbett made a name for himself as state Attorney General by investigating fraud and corruption. Yet, he refused to investigate why Unkovic resigned, which sparked rumors that he was forced out.

In a sloppily handwritten letter to the court, Unkovic said he did his best and wishes the citizens of Harrisburg well. "I have done my best to use my powers as receiver to bring fiscal stability to the City of Harrisburg. However, I find myself in an untenable position in the political and ethical crosswinds and am no longer in a position to effectuate a solution."

The main question everyone had now concerned those "political and ethical crosswinds." What did that mean?

With the city again on fire, Thompson attempted to assure residents of her leadership by embarking on a barnstorming town hall campaign. It didn't work.

Papst Reporter Intro from Mayor Town Hall:

Tonight, the Mayor held her 15th town hall meeting and second of the week to talk to residents and get her message out. These meetings have been sparsely attended. The one tonight only had about 10 people and I've been to others that only had two or three. And for some of the people who came tonight, the Mayor's town hall wasn't quite what they expected.

Reporter Package:

Ronald Chapel: Harrisburg Resident

"I'm hoping to get a little more insight into the Mayor's plan and why the Mayor feels the plan is the best thing for Harrisburg residents."

Dot Montaine: Harrisburg Resident

"I'm anxious to see what's happening and how I can help."

Dot Montaine and Ron Chapel are long-time Harrisburg residents who care about their hometown. So, when they heard the Mayor was holding a town hall meeting near their homes, they wanted to go. It was important for both of them to learn about the city and help in any way they can. They were both optimistic going into the meeting; but here is what they had to say afterwards.

Ronald Chapel: Harrisburg Resident

"As far as some of her words, especially some of her words as they pertain to some City Council members; I'll respectfully reserve my opinion about that." (Chapel visibly upset and disappointed.)

But some were not so reserved. Montaine got so upset at the meeting she left early.

Dot Montaine: Harrisburg Resident

"It was supposed to be a brief presentation on Act 47. We haven't gotten to it. We are still stuck back in 2010 and how everyone's abusing poor Linda. The past is gone and we need to get ready for the future to cope with where we're heading. We shouldn't be dwelling in the past with, 'I did this, and they did that to me and they are awful. And oh my goodness, poor me.' I'm not a councilor listening to a patient. I'm a citizen trying to save my city."
END SCRIPT

Before Unkovic abruptly resigned, he did leave everyone with a little gift. Prior to his departure, he reversed City Council's decision and reinstated the city's Director of Communications. The Mayor got to keep her spokesman.

12: THE REAL REED

PROFESSIONALLY, I FIND LITTLE more satisfying than that moment when a story that took months to write, research and investigate is finished. But I also find it equally as disheartening when the story is not entirely complete. Thus was the case with a series piece I first presented in mid-2012. I had everything required for strong storytelling. I had never-before-seen bank accounts. I had great sound from city officials. I had pages of court documents and telling judicial decisions. But what I didn't have was Stephen Reed.

He proved far more elusive than I assumed. Weeks before air, I frequented his home and office with zero success. Had I not known of recent sightings, I would have assumed he relocated. I couldn't even find evidence he was still alive. No mail. No footprints. No upkeep of his property.

Reed lived in an unimpressive row home end unit in the city's midtown section—affectionately referred to as the "gay-borhood." Of all the area homes, his needed the most attention. With chipped green paint and a slanted stoop, it did not strike me as the home of a man of such stature.

Every time I knocked on the door, paint chips would stick to my knuckles. I would have used the metal doorknocker had it not been stuck in rust. And there was no way to see inside. The front windows were blocked by curtains layered behind shutters. A series of necessary obstacles secured the back. The house lacked those certain qualities that made it a home. It had four exterior walls and a roof, but no noticeable soul.

His work office was quite different. After Reed left city hall, he started a consulting firm and rented space from a former city colleague. Fred Clark had a reputation all his own. A smooth talker with raging confidence and numerous ex-wives, he had a reputation in town for many things—few positive. Clark offered Reed much needed African American support as mayor. Post regime, Clark offered Reed top-shelf office space.

The two men worked out of a renovated 1842 home with bright bricks and striking red trim. Located on the riverbank, clients were regaled with dazzling views of the water or a steady line of young women who regularly ran by.

I had frequented Reed's office nearly as much as his home. I would walk in, make my way up the wood-carved stairs, admire the thick crown molding, and be told by the secretary at the top, "Mr. Reed is not available right now." I never believed her, but my options were limited. I didn't even know what room Reed occupied. Plus, I didn't feel making a scene would get me anywhere.

The day before my first Reed investigation was scheduled to air, my news director told me to try to contact Reed one more time. I figured it was a waste of time. He clearly was not interested in an interview. But I didn't argue.

"Do you want me to go in with you?" my photographer asked as we parked outside Reed's office building.

"Sure," I replied as I gathered my notebook and pen. "You should be there just in case." I opened the car door and stepped out. "One never knows."

Walking up the stoop towards the giant hardwood door, I got a weird feeling. A few nerves kicked in as I turned the brass knob and stepped inside. The high pitched squeak of the hinges sounded off alone. When the door closed behind us, it sealed in the silence. The place was empty. All the televisions and radios were off, as were the lights. If not for the sun struggling past the window curtains, it would have been completely black. Minus the florescent bulbs, the dark timber banister lacked its previous luster. As did the early 20th century stained moulding and wainscoting.

I shot a dubious glance at my photographer before proceeding upstairs. With each step, the staircase groaned a little louder. But there was no secretary at the top to hear it. I stuck my head inside the office and peaked around a few corners.

"There's no one here." My photog had already made his way to other offices on the floor.

It's been my understanding that walking into an open building is not trespassing until an owner or tenant tells you to leave. Any type of signage that reads, "keep out" or "no one beyond this point" is legally as binding as the owner sending a verbal warning. I saw no signs. No one had told us to leave. So, we continued deeper in the wood trim gorged home. With no competing sounds, every creak of the floor seemed to bounce continually off the walls.

One-by-one, we looked behind each door. Some were locked. Some were not. Towards the end of the hall, I came across a door that caught my attention. It was old, dark and heavily carved, just like the others. But this one contained a certain nameplate, Stephen R. Reed. I waved over my photographer. The door was not latched and slightly open—though not enough to see inside. I placed my hand on the door and gently pushed. The opening door slowly unveiled an amazing sight. It looked like a museum. The walls were ornate with antique paintings of famous battles and leaders of men. Displayed on a book case near the door appeared a pair of Colt revolvers resting in a leather holster. I couldn't help myself, so I pushed the door slightly further until it stuck on a thick wool rug.

The smell of cigarettes and antiquity rushed by my nose. The artifacts that filled the room left me stunned. I had heard rumors. But until now, I questioned their accuracy. Any doubts I had about my reportage had vanished.

"What do you see?" My photog stood behind me on look out.

I gripped the brass knob and carefully returned the door to its original position. "He's not here."

"I'm a little creeped out, man," he nearly whispered. "Let's get out of here."

As we followed the wooden banister back to the stairs, I heard a door swing open.

"Can I help you?" The voice came from behind us.

We turned to find a well-kempt man standing in the doorway we had just vacated. A hallow of smoke had yet to fully release from his lungs. The heavy light streaming from the rear windows slightly cast him in silhouette. Despite his feeble condition, he looked confident in his fragility.

"Mr. Reed," I began to approach him. "My name is Chris Papst, I'm a reporter for CBS 21 news."

"OK," he was not impressed. I could tell he didn't remember, or recognize, me from our first encounter. Or, perhaps he wasn't an avid local news viewer. "I have clients coming soon. What do you want?"

To my surprise, I found myself caught in a mild state of consternation. It was approaching two years since our previous encounter at the Civil War Museum. And during that time I had spent countless hours investigating him and conducting interviews concerning his legacy. It was odd to think standing before me was the focus of my obsession.

"Well." I swallowed. "We are doing a story tomorrow on your time as mayor," I tried to make my pitch as favorable to him as possible. "And I was wondering if you'd like to provide a comment."

I paused—waiting for a response that never came.

I continued, "We are discussing the Pottsville bank accounts you created and how you spent the money. We talk about the law suits you were involved in." I took a breath, having no idea what he was thinking. His stoic body language afforded me no clues. "I'd really like to get your side if you're willing to comment and..."

"I'm not interested," he interrupted. "You can leave now." He then disappeared into the smoke filled museum. The door latched behind him.

I dropped my head and shut my eyes. "Did you happen to roll on any of that?" I asked my photog.

"Not a frame," he said in earnest.

I spent the better part of the next 15 seconds staring blankly at the floor. I just blew my best chance to interview him. I recited the brief conversation, contemplating what I could have done differently. Maybe there was a better way to present myself. Maybe there wasn't. But either way, I failed. And I was pretty confident my upcoming stories wouldn't change his mind.

The next time I would see Stephen Reed I would be chasing him down a hallway. And unlike this time, he would know exactly who I was.

Anchor Intro:

The City of Harrisburg is facing huge financial challenges... and the situation is getting worse every day. Between the incinerator, retirement obligations and other contracts... the city now has a massive debt of $600 million... 12 times the city's annual operating budget. Tonight, we have shocking new information from a CBS 21 News investigation.

CBS 21's Chris Papst joins us live. Chris, how did this happen? What did you uncover?

Papst Reporter Intro:

Robb and Tanya, we uncovered some surprising bank records involving Mayor Reed's former financial dealings.

Stephen Reed was the Mayor of Harrisburg for 28 years. He was called "Mayor for life." He won elections by huge margins and at times ran unopposed. But in the aftermath of his administration, the city has financially collapsed, forcing City Council to file for bankruptcy and the state to take over.

And looking back, two judges and a former Dauphin County DA say former Mayor Reed exceeded the limits of his power... as mayor.

Package Report:

It was a time that Pennsylvania's capital city would like to forget. It was the early 1980s and the city was in bad shape; the population was fleeing; crime was high, and thousands of buildings were vacant. Its future looked bleak. But a new era was about to begin as Stephen Reed was elected. During his record 28 years as mayor, the city thrived... residents moved back, crime fell and employment increased. Hotels and museums were built; a University was founded and a baseball team came to town.

Neil Grover: Debt Watch Harrisburg

"There was a certain mythology that grew around him. He pulled us back from the brink and we seemed to move forward. And he was civil-minded when there was horrible things happening here."

But behind the ribbon cuttings, celebrations, handshakes, and smiles, a much different story was not being told. Dan Miller was on City Council at that time:

Dan Miller: Controller/ Former Council Member

"It's very similar to a dictator. Basically you had to toe the line or you were shut out. I wasn't necessarily on the inside, but because of two items [where we disagreed] I got completely shut out."

Karl Singleton was on the school board when Reed took it over. He says it was Reed's way... or no way...

Karl Singleton: Former School Board Member

"We were trying to put up barriers against the swap and bond transactions and we were summarily removed [from the process]. What we need is a true democracy, not a controlled democracy, which is how Steve Reed operated."

And the way Reed operated *was* challenged. In 1989, he was taken to court by City Council member Reizden Moore. Moore claimed Reed abused his power as mayor by entering into a contract with the Harrisburg Senators baseball team without the City Council's approval.

Today, the Senators are credited for revitalizing City Island. But did Reed abuse his power in how he brought the team here? The court ruled, yes. "The Mayor had no authority to negotiate contracts imposing financial burdens and obligations on the City of Harrisburg without the authority or approval of City Council." But the contracts already had been signed and the team was playing ball here. (Therefore, Reed was not disciplined.)

A few years later, Reed was back in court again... this time for setting up two bank accounts without the approval of City Council. This never-before-released document, acquired by CBS 21 news, and confirmed by the Harrisburg Authority, shows one of those accounts. Reed used $7 million from the sale of water bonds to open the account in 1990. As you can see, much of the money was used for big purchases, including bonds and t-notes worth upwards of $3.1 million.

But that's not all. The paperwork we obtained shows Reed also sent millions to another bank account in Pottsville. From this account, he also doled out huge amounts of money. So much money, Reed was sued and taken to court by 13 Harrisburg residents, claiming the Mayor abused his power by not getting City Council's approval. The residents won. In his decision, the late Judge Joseph Kleinfelter wrote, "[The Mayor] unlawfully usurped power vested in City Council." But, citing lack of authority, Kleinfelter said he would not, "fine the Mayor" ... as requested by the citizens' lawsuit.

"The Harrisburg 13" remain upset to this day. Pamela Parson is one of those 13.

Pamela Parson: "Harrisburg 13"

"It was a financial house of cards. We borrowed money to pay off borrowed money. Basically, it was a slap on the wrist; don't do it again. And he continued to do it in more and creative ways."

Reed's fiscal actions also caught the attention of the District Attorney at that time. DA Richard Lewis, now a sitting Dauphin County judge, investigated Reed in the 1990s and concluded, "The Mayor acted beyond the limits of his legal authority." But Lewis went on to say, "None of these improprieties appear to rise to the level of criminal conduct. [Reed] was motivated solely by what he saw to be the best interest of the city."

END SCRIPT

The response to that story was what I had hoped. People started talking, especially to me. And that led directly to my next piece, which answered the original question that started me on this path—why did Council vote 6-1 in favor of the incinerator retrofit when city residents were nearly unanimously opposed to it?

Anchor Intro:

In our continuing coverage of the Capital City in Crisis... As Harrisburg continues to fall deeper into this financial crisis, the state Senate wants to know how this happened. On Thursday the Senate will hold hearings on the incinerator and much of the attention is sure to focus on a City Council vote from 2003, which many consider the beginning of this crisis. Now, CBS 21 has discovered shocking new information that brings that vote into question. This is a story you will only see on CBS 21 news. CBS 21's Chris Papst is live with the Dauphin County Mobile Newsroom in Harrisburg with the details, Chris.

Papst Reporter Intro:

This has the potential of being a huge scandal and investigators are looking into it. Back in 2003, with the incinerator shut down, City Council—in a last ditch effort to save it—was offered a $120 million loan to repair it. At first, Council was reluctant to borrow the money. But Mayor Stephen Reed believed in the project and made deals with Council to get the loan approved. But it's *how* those deals were made that's being looked at.

Package Report:
Linda Thompson: Harrisburg Mayor

"I don't know whose vote he secured, but he didn't secure my vote. I cannot be bought by no penny or no million dollars. It would be arrogant of me to take a bribe and come back and run for the mayor."

That was Mayor Linda Thompson, responding to our questions about this—the recent forensic audit on the incinerator. This document, backed by 8000 pages of data, sheds new light on a vote by City Council in 2003 to fix the facility; within this report, CBS 21 found a brief email exchange that raises questions about what really happened.

The audit says when City Council members weren't onboard with the project they were offered $500,000 in cash for a "Special Projects Fund". An adviser to Mayor Stephen Reed wrote this in an email, "[Council President Richard House] will hold the vote until he hears from the Mayor. I understand Council is getting its money. So, the usual crap is flying." — Andy Giorgione, Harrisburg Authority Special Council

But when it appeared the vote may still fail, Mayor Reed responded with this email, "If all of you keep this up, you will permanently kill the prospect of the retrofit bonds being adopted by Council. With so little time available to this office, I find myself again having to edit and rewrite staff work products."

Also *right* before the vote, this email was sent referencing Harrisburg businessman Fred Clark and Reynolds Construction—which was hired to work on the incinerator: "Reynolds (and Freddie) are getting paid $1m and think they can deliver the votes."—Andy Giorgione, Harrisburg Authority Special Council

The question is, *how* were those votes delivered and where did that $1 million go?

Bill Cluck: Harrisburg Authority Board

"I think it's clear from the documents we obtained that someone needs to look at this."

Bill Cluck sits on the Harrisburg Authority Board, which released the audit. He says federal investigators need to subpoena people to get the truth because as eye-opening as the audit is, much information is still missing.

Bill Cluck: Harrisburg Authority Board

"It's been our understanding that former Mayor Reed's files disappeared from city hall during the transition (from Mayor Reed to Mayor Thompson). To me, if that is true, that's a violation of state law."

Back to Mayor Thompson, she was on City Council in 2003 and voted yes for the retrofit. When we pressed her on the series of emails we found in the audit, this is how she reacted.

Linda Thompson: Harrisburg Mayor

"We got no money in exchange for the vote, which is what you started out saying."

Papst: "That is what the audit says."

Linda Thompson: Harrisburg Mayor

"This is the end of my discussion." (She then turned her back and walked away.)

Papst Live Outcue:

When the loans were approved for the retrofit, millions of dollars were paid out in fees. So many people had a huge financial stake in the project.

END SCRIPT

Essentially, Harrisburg was sunk by bonds that should have never been issued. But now, I needed to know more about *why* they were issued. Without entering the psyche of those involved, most explanations would be speculation. But Council's bankruptcy attorney Mark Schwartz provided me with some convincing insight into the overall problem. As a young man, Schwartz worked for the bond agencies and worked with Reed in issuing much of the paper that killed the city. He answered my question in an email. These are his words:

"The U.S.'s providing a tax exemption for purchasers of debt issued by state and local governments for public purposes is another long standing Federal program which began with honorable intentions and ends in enormous inefficiencies and fraud. The idea is to provide a subsidy for such projects as schools, water systems, parking lots, roads, public buildings, dams and stadiums, making it cheaper to finance those projects without Congress having to make an appropriation for each project. Accordingly states, localities, authorities and non-profits are able to issue bonds for public purposes. These bonds are automatically exempt from state and Federal taxation. During the endless parade and charade of dealing with the extent of the public debt, talk always surfaces about eliminating the wasteful tax exemption with the billions of tax revenues that would follow. However, it is always talk. Bond issues need not be publicly bid. Pin-striped patronage is a much bigger deal than the blue collar patronage of the old days where campaign supporters were awarded low or no-show jobs in government. Politicians get elected from contributions made by bond participants. They get treated like royalty, being flown to New York and wined and dined at the most expensive restaurants, strip clubs, and showered with tickets to Broadway shows, concerts or every conceivable sporting event. Their friends and families are paid as consultants. And the politicians themselves can make a hefty multiple of their government salaries after leaving office simply to hook Wall Street up with those running Main Street who are able to float bond issues.

"Municipal bonds are not registered with the Securities and Exchange Commission and there is no pre-approval required. The argument made by the SEC is that it can regulate the underwriters when it comes to what is disclosed to bond purchasers, but that actually regulating issuance of debt would be an impermissible breach of 'states' rights.'

Over the last 50 years, bond offering prospectuses have gone from three pages in length to hundreds. Frankly they say less in terms of what a potential really wants to know when determining what bond to buy.

"Given the fact that the Federal government is subsidizing these bonds, it should have some say in the same way that it requires corporate offerings to be formally regis-tered. Besides, 'states' rights' was last in vogue in that wonderful era of the late 1950s and early 1960s when hooded Klansman and ax handles ruled the South and George Wallace proclaimed 'Segregation Now, Segregation Forever.' Oddly enough, this dubious empty mantle has been raised by the National Conference of State Legislatures, the League of Municipalities and the State Treasurers' Association. Of course, the real rationale deals not with seeking to limit an already limitless Federal government. Nor is the goal efficient when it comes to public finance. To the contrary it has everything to do with fundamental and personal needs of politicians when it comes to raking in millions in campaign finances.

"Whether a bond issue is legal has more to do with the herd psychology of a small and highly-paid cadres of bond lawyers who sign legal opinions approving each issuance, and less to do with strict adherence to statute or regulation. Subjective requirements like 'public facilities,' 'reasonable expectations' and 'maintenance or creation of jobs' allow fee hungry lawyers and bankers to create complex deals that defy common sense. Besides, they don't get paid to say 'no' to a bond issue. A 'yes' answer often commonly brings six figures to the lawyers and seven or more to the bankers.

"One would think that credit rating agencies would police the municipal bond market. To some degree they do. However, they too depend on fees from deals also miss a lot when it comes to due diligence. The name of the game is for states, cities or towns to have an investment grade rating so that certain funds and institutions can purchase the bonds for their portfolios. Municipal issuers are given credit ratings by the rating agencies. The problem is that those states and towns with not such great credit ratings can purchase an investment grade rating by purchasing bond insurance. The credit of the insurance company is substituted for the poor credit of a city or town. All it takes is the payment of an insurance premium based on the size of the borrowing, which of course comes out of the bond issue. Until the last several years, bond insurers made a fortune charging six figure fees and never having to pay out. Bond insurance was a cash cow, until now. One would think that an insurance company that charged a premium would suck it up and pay up, but actually they look for recourse against the city or town that borrowed the money and paid the premium. They want to do anything but continue to pay bond holders. That is why they hired the law firm previously headed by the Governor's in-house lawyer to lobby the Legislature, block a bankruptcy and impose a receiver who wants to put it all on the backs of taxpayers.

"There is also the unique nature of the earnings on municipal bond proceeds, before they are spent: 'municipal bond arbitrage.' There is big money to be earned by reinvesting the money raised, as opposed to spending it, on an actual project. Because these bonds are tax-exempt they carry a lower interest rate than corporate bonds or commercial loans. Traditionally, tax exempt interest rates have traditionally been less than half of prevailing interest rates. Thus there is always a temptation to borrow the money and not spend it, but instead earn 'arbitrage': the spread between the tax exempt and taxable rates. For example, on a hundred million dollars in bond proceeds raised, the cost of carrying the debt is say three million (3%) while almost six million (6%) can be made by reinvesting the proceeds in available securities.

"This 'free money' is what paid for Harrisburg's redevelopment [under Reed] from getting an island transformed to an amusement and minor league baseball venue to a Hilton Hotel. Millions in arbitrage also balanced the budget. That was before the IRS severely limited the practice in the 1986 Tax Act.

"However, it's always been a creative game where bond lawyers and investment bankers end-run the IRS which, only periodically comes down on some in 'whack-a-mole' fashion putting the kabosh on one particular scheme while three or four others immediately pop up to replace it. It's all about exploiting arbitrage and raiding the treasury.

"Harrisburg's 'Mayor for Life,' Stephen Reed, may have been untouched when it came to being attracted and ulti-mately addicted to arbitrage. Forget political contributions, although many underwriters made them anyway. He had an open door policy for any underwriter which could generate fees and earnings for the city, regardless of whether there was real project. Traditional logic has it that financings come after a project is defined. Wrong. Financings themselves became an end for projects that could be dummied up to exist in name only. This was all done directly by the city or for the host of municipal authorities he created and controlled. Hundreds of millions, perhaps billions of dollars of bonds were issued for projects that would never be built; financings structured in such a way as to not allow the bond proceeds to be spent on brick and mortar, but to virtually all be locked into higher yielding investments.

"Take for example, the then humongous $300 million Harrisburg Hydro-Electric Dam project of the early 1980s, which was to transform the listless three-foot-deep Susquehanna River into a raging force of nature from which cheap electricity would be harnessed. The end of the Arab oil cartel and filthy coal firing plants were immediately within grasp. All that it took was a 'feasibility study' from a connected engineering firm; another seem-ingly open term for what is really nothing more than a purchased foregone conclusion. Then with nothing much more than the pen of a connected bond lawyer, the city, not to mention the deal participants, would be awash in money. And an initial $300 million hydroelectric deal would be refinanced several more times. The lion's share of the $300 million was never spent. It, along with a small amount of the 'arbitrage' earned, paid off the bonds and bond interest owed as they became due. Investors were made whole. Underwriters and consultants made millions with each deal and the city had a huge windfall of cash: manna from heaven (actually from the U.S. Treasury).

"After the excesses of the 1980s, it seemed like Mayor Reed was a bond addict, as he went museum crazy in his conviction to make Harrisburg a first class destination city. First, there was a Civil War Museum. Next there was to be a Wild West Museum. Never mind Harrisburg's eastern location, at least the project fulfilled the Mayor's passion for shopping, as he personally made the acquisitions, many of them overpriced and allegedly phony. What is more a signature development project [David Dodd] went belly up, leaving a partially completed office complex with empty window casements and cheap siding blowing in the wind. Perhaps he had in mind a public memorial or museum of contractor rip offs and failed redevelopment.

"City budgets had become a shell game balanced by inter-fund borrowings and bond proceeds. Perhaps only former Mayor Reed knows where the money came from and what it was originally obligated towards."

Basically, what Schwartz is saying is Harrisburg was allowed to pay one credit card with another. And, as long as Wall Street continued to make new lines of credit available for the city, politically connected lawyers, consultants and bankers got paid millions. But when what is fake becomes real, and the bills come due, you get Harrisburg.

The reports and research presented in this chapter offered many answers to what happened to Harrisburg. But there was still one question that continued to nag me. Why would a man who regularly brokered hundred million dollar bond deals, while scrapping off millions for secret bank accounts and personally enriching untold numbers of professionals and personal friends over the duration of his administration, live in such a mediocre and run-down home? I got the possible answer via one five-minute phone conversation.

The call came from a source with first-hand knowledge of an event that took place just a few days prior. He told me that Reed had been out of town when his house alarm had been set off. By law, police were allowed to enter the home. While inside the home, they found a virtual museum of historical artifacts—many of which were Wild West themed. From the basement to the attic, I was told boxes stuffed the home. Some were open, some weren't. Some rooms and hallway barely had enough room to allow for walking. I was told those artifacts on display truly belonged behind glass.

The officers took pictures. But fearing the loss of their jobs or pensions, they chose not to hand them over. I thought I could link some of the artifacts to ones I knew Reed bought specifically for the city. But I never got the chance. I also never would have thought such impressive items would have existed in such an unimpressive home.

13: SCUMBAGS

BY MARCH 27TH, 2013, Mayor Linda Thompson was well into her third year as mayor and running for re-election. The Democratic primary was just a few months away and the polls were not incumbent-heavy. The state was still in control. The city's debts were still not being paid and no recovery plan was in place. To bolster her case for a second term, Thompson needed a spark. She needed to find a way to get the electorate's attention. She needed a conduit in which to display her leadership and build the appropriate momentum ahead of Election Day. And she sought that catalyst in trash. So on that latter March morning, she called for a press conference.

Trash had been a longstanding issue for the city. It blocked sidewalks, clogged storm drains and covered streets. It was so pervasive, it was often taken for granted and overlooked. It simply became a part of everyday life. With the blight, poverty and crime, random piles of trash fit right in.

Media-wise, trash is not a sexy topic, especially for the overwhelming majority of our suburban viewership that doesn't need further reason to avoid city life. But on this day, the Mayor's podium was half surrounded by cameras.

And similar to most other days, this was not due to the topic but rather the Mayor. We had been trained to follow Thompson's every public move. It was a strategy that worked countless times. Her hijinks had already earned her a spot on a national "worst persons" list. And what she was about to say on this day would garner her more national attention.

Exiting the elevator, Thompson approached the stand with large pearls matching a black-specked tweed jacket. The presser focused on the privatization of waste collection, during which Thompson lamented the illegal dumping that further defaced the capital. It was assumed some of the "perps" were out-of-towners who would simply ditch their bulk items and flee. When the discussion shifted to opening up the incinerator for a free day of trash disposal for city residents, the Mayor delivered media magic.

In an unnecessarily harsh and unforgiving voice, she barked: "We're not opening up our flood gates for some scumbag from Perry County who got the money and pocketed it, and comes here and wants to dump it for free."

What followed was a political shit-storm, the likes of which I have never seen. Right after this quote, every media outlet in central Pennsylvania raced to Perry County for comment. After all, Perry County is Harrisburg's direct neighbor to the north. Prior to this moment, the two existed in harmony. The harmony died.

"I've heard her say some really dumb things during her tenure. But this has to be the dumbest," one Perry County resident told me.

"We do a lot of work and put a lot of money into that city. We work there, pay taxes and pay to park. It's wrong," added another in disbelief.

Elected county officials were not silent, either.

"You just don't expect to hear that sort of offensive and crude talk from a city leader," added a Perry County commissioner.

The county's state Representative told media his legislative emails "blew up" following that remark. "I take offense to that comment. It is so far out of line. It's totally ridiculous."

The mayor of one of Perry County's largest municipalities opined, "When you make a brazen attack like that and use words that are so inappropriate, it's going to be very personal. I think especially in a city with so many problems, you would be a little more humble and focus on the issues that are substantial."

An enraged cadre demanded Thompson apologize. A Facebook page demanding her impeachment quickly tallied 5,000 likes, in a county of 45,000 people. A corresponding Facebook page defending Thompson sported 63 likes.

The fallout took on a life of its own as Perry County residents, who are nearly unanimously rural, German and Italian, evolved to embrace her comment. Local eateries started making "scumbag pizza" pepperoni, ham, sausage, green peppers, onions and mushrooms that sold for $12.99. One dollar from each pie went to the Perry County Shelter. A variety of scumbag t-shirts went on sale ranging from $10-$14. Some featured Thompson's likeness with the words "OoOops My BAD!!," while others read, "Property: Perry County Scumbag. Est. 2013 XXL" These proceeds went to a library and playground.

Storefronts, flea markets, beer stores and gas stations made signs welcoming Scumbags for business. "Support Perry County Scumbags." A music video "Perry County Scumbag Thrift Shop" appeared on YouTube openly mocking the Mayor. It got more than 10,000 views. I admit, a few were me. What can I say? It has a good beat.

When Thompson finally issued an apology, she stayed true to her own caricature by penning it in the third person. "The Mayor's reference specifically to illegal dumpers from Perry County has been distorted out of (context). Obviously the Mayor was not referring to the citizens of Perry County. Many of the city's workers, visitors and friends come from Perry County into the city every day and the city has a long, positive relationship with the county. The Mayor apologizes to the good citizens of Perry County for any negative connotation implied in her comments on fighting blight in the city."

Her words further damaged the city financially when one of the Perry County's largest boroughs pulled its trash contract. The borough manager released this statement concerning the decision:

"The recent comments made by Harrisburg Mayor Thompson regarding Perry County people hauling trash to Harrisburg initiated a discussion of the Borough's current vendors accepting trash from the Borough.

"The Borough records reflect that in the fiscal year 2012, Duncannon Borough paid over $49,000 to the Harrisburg Incinerator.

"Since Mayor Thompson suggested that the Borough was not welcome to bring Perry County trash to Harrisburg, the Borough has since contracted with another provider at a lesser cost which it believes will alleviate a portion of the Mayor's expressed concerns. It will also save our rate payers unnecessary costs of service.

"We thank Mayor Thompson for calling this to our attention. We had no idea the Harrisburg Incinerator did not want our business and are pleased to announce that we have taken steps to accommodate Mayor Thompson's wishes."

Thompson's scumbag comment earned her a spot on Time Magazine's list of ten mayors on "a road to political purgatory." She landed that coveted spot right next to Toronto's Rob Ford.

It was antics like this, month after month, that drew the public's venomous ire. It wasn't long before someone started making highly insulting internet cartoons with pithy titles such as "Linda talk Payroll", "Linda and the

Beavers" and "Linda Vs the Angry Mob." Feel free to watch them on YouTube. I was never able to uncover the identity of the creator, upongreenstreet. But, they are excellently produced and grew to be quite popular.

Check out these comments concerning the Mayor. They appeared on a Facebook post for a local news station (Fox 43, May 16, 2011). Here's the story. Thompson twice sued the "homosexual, evil little" Controller, saddling taxpayers with thousands in lawyer fees. The first was over the issuance of direct deposit paychecks for city employees and the second was over the Controller's refusal to sign off on the Wild West Artifacts auction. Following the second suit, the people sounded off.

"It amazes me how she continually 'manages' to out asshole herself almost on a regular basis."

"The biggest joke of a mayor in the nation resides in the capital of Pennsylvania."

"Resign you stupid moron. Nobody wants you the Mayor of Harrisburg."

"I truly believe she would do better as a KFC manager than mayor."

"@Edwin: She would do better as the cook."

"Someone must have assaulted her with the ugly stick... you could show a movie on that forehead of hers."

"Dan Miller should sue her for slander—her racist and anti-gay comments are even on record."

"It would be nice if she would focus all her energy into fixing our capital city instead of continuing to mock it!!"

"I am so sick of hearing the name Linda Thompson in the news. She is the drama queen of local politics."

This was just one day and one thread and not one comment was positive. And it was like this every day in every media outlet. It started the moment she took office and persisted throughout the length of her administration. At first, I tried very hard to be fair to her. I felt bad for her. Harrisburg's collapse was not her fault. She was placed in a situation for which she was ill-prepared. Personally, I don't think she had any clue how bad city finances were upon taking office, even though she was City Council president. Perhaps no one did, except Stephen Reed.

As much as I tried to give her the benefit of the proverbial double, over time I did find myself trying less. Whatever "it" is she didn't get it and didn't seem to want to get it. Just when I thought she couldn't further disappoint, she'd reach new heights. Perhaps the most positive aspect of her administration lay in its entertainment value. Every time I left the city, someone was bound to express their joy in watching the Mayor on TV. I'm sure she helped our ratings.

Here are more of the moments that made her a household name.

After it was first reported that Thompson referred to the Controller as a "Homosexual evil little man," a Harrisburg resident called her asking for an explanation. Thompson ended up calling him back and left a rambling four-minute message, which made little sense. The man, of course, took the message to the media. She began her third-person soliloquy with pleasantries, "Hi, Mr. Pierre MaCoy, how are you? Your message warrants a direct and personal call from the Mayor. This is the Mayor of the City of Harrisburg."

In the message she referred to the political climate in Harrisburg as a war that is full of evil. She said people are plotting against her. "You can best believe this is not my character. This is being orchestrated by a few people and most of them are a group of men in a certain section of town that were either campaign managers and/or candidates in the mayoral race that I happen to defeat." At this point, her delivery began to swell in volume and pace. "I have done incredible work in this administration. But the Patriot News refuses to give it the time and the day in the Patriot News because they want to sell newspapers. Please, have faith in me. And do not get your facts in the paper because it does not have your interest at heart."

The man said the Mayor never answered his actual question. "I can assure you that I am a woman who has a passion for all people, Mr. MaCoy. And under no circumstances did I make those, as you deem to be, derogatory comments in the context in which The Patriot-News is writing." She also discussed the mass exodus of her staffers and concluded by expressing that, "All is well. And no matter who is leaving this administration, they are jumping ship because they know there is much stuff to be done. And they can't prove that they've done things, even under Steve Reed's leadership."

One time, City Council's lone white member, Brad Koplinski, questioned Thompson's actions during public bids for city work. In response, she created a stack of favorable posters and called a presser to say, "If Mr. Koplinski yells one more time that the Mayor didn't want a public bid, all of you should arrest him." Perhaps she confused the media with the police. We carry cameras and microphones. No handcuffs.

"Only God can fix the financial mess of the city. Man cannot fix the financial state of the city." That one comment got Thompson in mild trouble with some local atheists. Her three-day fast and prayer got her in slightly more trouble with Current TV's Keith Olbermann. But years of these types of public displays of faith eventually caught the attention of larger outside atheist groups. And with those larger groups came larger trouble.

While the atheists didn't seem to have a problem with Thompson celebrating her faith, they did have a problem with her doing so while in her capacity as mayor. The atheists put forth, "Thompson says she depends on God for guidance, but this has failed in the past because Harrisburg is facing a tremendous financial crisis unless, of course, God exists and doesn't like Harrisburg." David Silverman, president of American Atheists, called Thompson's actions a "complete violation of common sense, not only church and state" and also noted "it is not responsible of the Mayor to preach religion."

On numerous occasions Thompson would brag, "I am history. [I am the] first African American woman to ever seize the office of the Mayor and the first woman."

She once declared during a City Council meeting, "The Mayor needs to get out, ladies and gentlemen. I've sacrificed the entire year, and I haven't been able to get out."

In the midst of Thompson's feud with Council, she told the media, "I'm hoping that Council was more willing to be on the champion team of the Mayor as opposed to the failed team."

She once said of her ability to govern, "You gotta be able to multi-task and multi-manage. I take out the trash sometimes."

Thompson once attended a ribbon cutting ceremony at the Boys and Girls Club and blatantly parked illegally in front of a fire hydrant.

At a time when Thompson implored residents to pay their real-estate taxes and other fees on time to help the struggling city, it was revealed she was delinquent in paying her own taxes. At a town hall meeting following the news a man stood up. "What's the deal, Mayor? You're defaulting on your loans when you say we shouldn't default on our loans?" Thompson, who made $80,000 a year as mayor, responded by saying she's "human" and that the personal financial problems she encountered didn't affect her ability to lead the city. A local bank had issued a foreclosure on a city house she owned where she ran Loveship Inc., which was some sort of non-profit that counseled people on their mortgages. She ran the company before becoming mayor. Thompson now owed $1,086 in property taxes according to the County Tax Claims Bureau.

She refused to apologize for her perceived hypocrisy. "I didn't file for bankruptcy [for the city] and I don't plan on filing for bankruptcy in my personal life. My property taxes, I'm on a payment plan. I encourage people to get on a payment plan. It's a tough job. I'm into my second year and whether you think I did a good job or not, I sleep well at night. I'm not this crazy erratic woman with these obstructionist looks in the paper."

When Thompson ran for re-election, she had few supports. One of them just happened to be Al Sharpton. At a conference in Harrisburg, in front of about 100 people he publicly endorsed her for a second term. "There is no place more important than what you do in Pennsylvania. Everything you face, nobody should have to convince you to come out this year [to vote]. The man talked about it in 1963 when Doctor King was in jail, people died to give us the right to vote. Here you are 40 years later in Harrisburg... just too lazy and ungrateful to use what others paid the price to give you. And there is not an elected official in the country that I know, that has more brains, courage and tenacity than your Mayor, Linda Thompson. And if we can't stand up and protect those who protect us, then there's something wrong with us. It's not about whether you (sic) on they (sic) side, it's whether you (sic) on your own side. For years, you had a 'Mayor for Life.' Now you have a black woman for mayor, and insecure black men try to tear her down. When the others were in, you had nothing to say. When a woman gets in, all of a sudden you find your manhood. You are nothing but dividers and enemies of progress. I mean, when did you discover your guts? You didn't discover your guts before. I say what I've got to say. I'm tired of every time our children get someone to look up to, out of pettiness we tear them down."

Following the Trayvon Martin verdict, Thompson attended a rally in Harrisburg and pronounced, "Every person out there who possesses a gun illegally, put that gun away in the name of Trayvon Martin, so there's no more black on black crime. We believe George Zimmerman is guilty of intentionally killing Trayvon Martin. We want to make sure we continue to raise the conscience levels of people so they can make sure they are actively involved in voting and voting for the right judges."

Coincidentally, weeks before this rally, a man Theodore Meriweather shot and killed another man, John Lumpkins in Harrisburg. Meriweather claimed self-defense after Lumpkins attacked him downtown. Meriweather was charged with murder. It was very similar to the Martin situation except both men were black. When I asked Thompson about these charges in reference to the self-defense claims of George Zimmerman, she responded, "I don't really have a comment on that. I don't know what happened, there. We'll trust the district attorney." The charges against Meriweather were later dropped when his self-defense claim was validated. Thompson didn't protest.

These were some of the Mayor's words after the Eastern Sports and Outdoor Show was cancelled in January, 2012. "This controversy [was] caused by firearms manufacturers who profit from the sale of weapons designed for the mass killing of human beings." The massive exposition had been held annually since 1955 at Harrisburg's Farm Show Complex. Shortly after the Sandy Hook shooting, the British company that ran the show banned the sale of "assault rifles" or "modern sporting rifles." This triggered (sorry) a boycott that ultimately led to the show's canceling. With 1200 dealers and tens of thousands of visitors over nine days, it was considered the largest show of its kind in North America. Its cancellation costs the local economy an estimated $80 million. But instead of Thompson fighting to save the show which local restaurants, vendors and hotels depended on, she decided to use the opportunity to highlight the negative impact of illegal gun violence. "Too many urban city kids have died and that's the message going forward that we are one voice going forward. The city is still open for business and still doing business. And if the gun show pulls out it's not going to put a huge dent in our economic face. We have existing retail shops, restaurants, hotels, lobbying groups. We have insurance companies. We have hospitals. We have schools. We have our very own federal government, state government, city and county government. I think we are doing well without a gun show. We don't want to lose any business. But there are some things you just don't want to align yourself with. We are banding together to make sure we divest in any company that is producing armor pellet guns (her actual term) that will kill a police officer" (Roxbury News). She went on to say gun companies operate in a manner that is inhumane.

14: REED'S RATIONALE

WITH THE AUTUMN OF 2012 APPROACHING, city spirits remained low. The recovery process appeared to have stalled. Though, the city's collapse had not. The longer a plan took to finalize, many more millions of debt would have to be addressed. Fatigue had set in for just about everyone, including the criminals. The alarming spike in violence that defined the year's inception had tailed off. Apparently, most everyone was giving up and losing interest.

And amazingly, throughout this entire ordeal, the man most responsible had succeeded in avoiding media attention. It had been two years since Stephen Reed's speech at the Civil War Museum. Therefore, it had been two years since his last public appearance. The Mayor who was everywhere was suddenly the resident who was nowhere. Occasionally, I would get a tip he was spotted along restaurant row (a few blocks of bars and restaurants downtown that were of his creation) but by the time I arrived he'd be gone.

But all this was about to change. Earlier that year, the Harrisburg Authority, the entity that owns the incinerator, released a forensic audit detailing how the project went awry. This audit was the basis of my report on Reed and how he got deals done. It discussed the "special projects fund" and contained questionable emails concerning intent between interested parties.

The Pennsylvania Senate Committee on Local Government took notice of the audit and called for a series of hearings to discuss it. The goal was to learn exactly what Harrisburg did wrong to accumulate $350 million in debt for a facility that had a value a third that amount. The men most involved in the debacle were called to answer questions. These men, who had been able to successfully avoid any semblance of culpability, were now forced to speak on the record and under oath. And these men included Stephen Reed.

City advocates could smell blood. The incinerator debt was the main culprit of Harrisburg's misfortune. The decisions surrounding its operation ruined Pennsylvania's capital. Now, one-by-one, those most responsible would parade themselves in front of the world to answer for their actions—and many hoped, their crimes. Within the media and local political circles, this was the Super Bowl of, what are normally boring and otherwise meaningless, Senate hearings.

The day that Reed was scheduled to testify, I arrived to the Capitol early. Most everyone did. The light banter in the hallway prior to the gavel drop seemed to carry with it a certain excitement. The hearing was held in a Senate room with plenty of seating and additional standing room. Many of the city's current and previous officials were present. The audience also contained those who would run for office in the coming months.

Sitting directly behind Reed's eventual chair, sat the man who in a year's time would be the next mayor. The current mayor didn't find it important enough to show up.

Reed arrived not a second early—allowing him to traverse through an empty hallway. Everyone had already claimed their seats inside. Had there been a popcorn machine, I got the impression most everyone would have indulged.

When Reed approached the bar, he walked lightly and gently opened the gate. With a pressed black suit and tan tie, he appeared comfortable given the environment. Although, a certain aspect of his being appeared disinterested and unsure of why he was even there.

Once inside the bar, he carefully leaned his blue and white umbrella against the rail. Few talked, though all watched. As he gradually situated himself, the dim fluorescent lighting flickered off the American flag pin attached to his lapel.

With thin gray hair and deep bags tugging at his eyes, the icon appeared beyond tired. Frail and hunched, he carried a worn countenance. But as he raised his right hand, his spine arched.

"Do you swear to tell the truth, the whole truth and nothing but the truth, so help you God?" The ranking Senator asked.

"I do so swear."

And with that, it was on.

Reed sat down in the defendant's chair. After securing his wire glasses, he read his opening remarks, which he claimed to have penned that morning. He explained how the EPA in Washington mandated the incinerator be retrofitted. And how a plan was drafted and heavily reviewed by the county, city and Harrisburg Authority which all hired their own "independent" engineering firms to review the project. He discussed the state's involvement. But what he did not explain were how so many "experts" didn't see the obvious flaws.

We now know the technology proposed to retrofit the incinerator was unproven, as was the contractor hired to install it. Yet, the project was still allowed to move forward without a performance bond. A performance bond is an insurance policy for public works projects, designed to protect the taxpayer. Reed claimed he did not know of the lack of a performance bond. Apparently, the Mayor who had his hands in everything was somehow hands off when it came to this aspect of the largest project the city ever undertook.

Reed blamed the failures on the inaccurate cost projections. "To this day I have never heard a complete answer to this question." He claimed the initial cost estimates appeared so sound they were never challenged at public hearings or meetings. Which was not true. Remember my story on the Council vote from 2003? The public was nearly unanimously opposed to the project and residents implored Council to reject the retrofit saying the cost estimates were wrong. These correct residents were subsequently called liars by Reed's spokesman.

"There was not a question of project costs being too low during the decision-making process," Reed told the Senators. "Had there been. Had the much higher project costs been known at the outset, I think it's pretty accurate to say this project would not have been started."

After Reed admitted the technology was beyond his expertise, he offered the Senators some advice. He boldly suggested the Local Government Debt Act, within the Department of Community and Economic Development, be amended to prevent future calamity. He said the current act lacked specifications for unique projects such as waste disposal incineration.

He called for a detailed state review featuring hired experts specialized in the particular field. To negate costs to taxpayers, those proposing the plans would pay for the application. He also suggested the Local Debt Act be amended to further scrutinize self-liquidating projects. Self-liquidating debt is debt that essentially pays for itself via increased revenue streams from the indebted project. The incinerator retrofit was sold to the public as self-liquidating to ensure the passage of the bonds (more on this later).

As Reed was offering this second bit of advice, the blue and white umbrella he had rested on the railing succumbed to gravity. It fell three feet and slammed against the laminate floor. A piercing crack echoed throughout the all-wood chamber. Reed glanced down at the floor, but never missed a beat in cadence or thought. The man was focused and could not be distracted.

When Reed finished his opening statement, the Senators pounced. They first pointed to an audit that specifically said the debt would not be self-liquidating—an obvious truth as the incinerator was now $350 million in debt. As he listened to subtle assumptions of his dishonesty, he remained calm to the point of disinterest. His responses were pithy and passionately vague. He took no blame and appeared to genuinely believe he was void of responsibility.

When asked about the continual dumping of money in the hapless facility, he said, "Do you complete the project so there is a revenue producing asset in place, or do you simply stop the project and it would never be completed? The decision was to finish the project." That answer somehow held up even after the original contractor went bankrupt and failed to finish the work. Remember the term "performance bond." This is when that would have come in handy.

Up to this point, Reed was able to simply talk his way through the hearing. He had received no direct hits and remained unscathed. Now, it was time for the panel to ask the "Mayor for Life" that one question that the audience had wanted to ask him for years.

"It seems no one did anything wrong? If that's true, how did the city, Authority, and county end up with the huge financial challenges they are now facing?" one Senator asked.

Reed replied in full confidence, "Because, the initial cost estimate to retrofit and expand the Harrisburg resource recovery facility was significantly under-estimated." He paused. "That is the genesis of all of this."

How disappointing an answer. You could feel the room dishearten. And the Senators didn't follow up with probing questions or statements—a further disappointment.

The forensic audit contained damning information that could be used to directly challenge what Reed had just said (more on this later, as well). But no challenge was issued.

The next set of questions focused on the millions of dollars in fees collected during the bond transfers. Reed claimed they went to the employees of the incinerator.

One Senator cited evidence in the forensic audit that said the money actually went into a "special projects fund" that the Mayor controlled and used for Wild West artifacts.

"From the city's [bond] fee? That's news to me." This was the only part of the hearing in which Reed appeared a little uncomfortable. "I don't know and I don't remember seeing that, frankly." In a rare moment of animation, he emphasized his point by firing both index fingers at the Senator—as if they were six-shooters.

"My view is that municipal government should not own and operate such a facility," Reed explained. "It should be in the public sector where there are efficiencies that government cannot create."

Even though Reed apparently felt the facility should be privately owned, he failed to make it so in his 28 years. In 1993, Mayor Reed sold the incinerator to the Harrisburg Authority, which is supposed to be an independent entity of the city. But as mayor, Reed appointed the board members. And according to the forensic audit, even though he didn't find it necessary to own the incinerator, he didn't have a problem spending the fees from its bond issuances.

At one point, Reed did seem to place partial blame on the county. He explained how the commissioners wanted to avoid re-opening a controversial landfill and the incinerator was their best option in that endeavor. I wonder if the county's "independent engineering firm" was aware of its client's desire to make the project work? Either way, county taxpayers were now responsible for about $125 million in debt.

The Senators also asked Reed to explain these "special project funds" he created. He said the Authority and the Mayor each had one to spend on projects outside the purview of their specific tasks. He firmly stated the Authority fund was under control of only Authority Board members. Oddly, he failed to mention the board members were all appointed by him. One of which later offered him prime office space along the river. I have been told that prime office space was offered to Reed rent-free. Though, I was never able to confirm that. The involved parties were less than willing to make public financial records.

With Reed still testifying, my photographer tapped me on the shoulder. He pointed at this camera. The battery was dying.

"Do you have another in the truck?" I whispered.

He nodded.

"Hurry up."

It seemed like the second he stepped out of the room, the Senators announced they had concluded their questioning. Reed quickly stood up, handed the panel his opening statement and exited the courtroom much faster than he had entered.

I snatched the microphone out of the bag, ripped camera off the tripod and took off after him. As I entered the hall, he had already made his way up the stairs towards the door.

"Mayor Reed!" I called out while giving chase. "Chris Papst from CBS 21 news."

He turned, but kept walking. A few media followed out the door behind me. I rushed as quickly as I could without running.

"Sir, can we asked you a few questions about your testimony?"

As I hurriedly approached, he turned and jabbed his boney finger at my face.

"You're that reporter!" I had never been scowled at in such a friendly way. "You're the one doing those stories on me."

"Yes, sir." I desperately didn't want to lose another interview with him. I had to be careful. I may not ever get another chance.

"Do you know how much you've hurt my business? You cost me a lot of clients."

Despite his aggressive advance, I kept my voice soft. "I am sorry to hear that, Mayor. That was not my intent." By this time numerous media outlets had partially surrounded him. I was confident he wouldn't reject us all. And I was right. One of those newly arrived reporters asked the first question. With that, the interview I had waited years for, had begun.

Reed started by answering a few questions about his testimony. The legends surrounding his charm were accurate. Even as he spoke of his decisions that destroyed Harrisburg while enriching a few, I found myself wanting to like him. Though, when I saw an opening, I fired out my first question.

"Why did so much money go to professionals?" I blurted out. "Up to $15 million dollars was paid out in fees that didn't go to the incinerator."

His answer was quick. "It's very common during large transactions for there to be a variety of lawyers, engineers and others, all of whom are supposed to perform different functions with the capital market transaction. If you don't have those folks doing that work, the bonds cannot be sold."

Another reporter quickly pointed out the technology placed in the incinerator didn't work and the operator had to rip out everything. Did the professionals really do their jobs?

"That is news to me," he replied. "Guys, I really have to go."

Before he turned away, I shouted. "Mayor, you acknowledged in the hearing this is a crisis. There are clearly many things you did for this city that were positive. What do you want to say to the people of Harrisburg now that they are going through all this."

I fully expected a complete answer. I didn't expect a history lesson.

"The current issue," he explained in earnest, "while it is significant in the size of the debt, can be solved. And the plans to solve this issue have been around for five or six years. There would be no incinerator debt issue today had we not been blocked from carrying forth our efforts to wipe out that debt. What was that plan?

"First, it was to long-term lease the Harrisburg Parking Authority assets. We got a $250 million offer to long term lease the Harrisburg Parking Authority assets, that would have not only retired all the Parking Authority bonds, but then you would have had substantial amounts to apply towards the incinerator debt. The second step was to sell the incinerator itself. We thought we'd get about $125 million. Once it's complete and up and operating it becomes a marketable item. The combination of that would have wiped out most of the incinerator debt.

"At that point, you go to the bond holders and make a what is called a tender offer. And say we are going to have trouble paying these bonds in the future. We will pay you 82 or 85 cents on the dollar right now. We can give you 85 cents on the dollar, right now! Most of them would have accepted that offer. If there were any that didn't, the understanding with the county was they would increase the tipping fee (per ton disposal costs) over a 10-year period of time to amortize the remaining debt.

"Bottom line is all of the incinerator debt, all of it, could have been wiped out five or six years ago. There has always been a solution to this. What has blocked it is the politics of doing nothing. A Washington political playbook gambit of 'why solve an issue if you can run on it?' None of the current circumstance would have existed today had we not been blocked in wiping out that incinerator debt five years ago."

This was a blatant swing at current city leadership. Take a guess who led Council's charge to reject the plan Reed just laid out? Why, Linda Thompson, of course. She along with the "evil" Controller Dan Miller spoke out against Reed's plan. What odd allies—allies that both ran for higher office after battling Reed and his plan to eliminate the debt.

During the length of this interview Reed insisted he had to go but always stuck around for another good laugh.

"That was funny," he said in reminiscence to a reporter question. "This reminds me of the old days." You could tell he relished the attention. And he had the charm turned way up. He seemed like a guy who'd have great stories to share at the local tavern. And I found myself wanting to hear those stories.

"What was I talking about?" He squinted in digression. "Ah, yes."

He returned to a serious tone. "We got within an inch of getting this done, and then Council passed a resolution saying they weren't going to take action at this time, and they would come up with an alternative." Yet, no alternative was ever presented. "Guys, I really have to go."

But before he could pull himself away, he was asked one last question. This one centered on the financial bond transactions he executed and his methods of using interest rate swaps to generate revenue.

A "swap" is a financial transaction where future interest payments on money owed is exchanged for another, where fixed rates are usually exchanged for an adjustable rate. They are very risky. But in explaining his methodology Reed may have revealed his true hand of intention.

"The Harrisburg Authority made millions of dollars on those swaps," he sternly pointed out.

And it was those millions, rather by swaps or by the bond issuances themselves, he used to help fund his many projects. It had finally all come together: the bonds issued during the incinerator retrofit, the allegations of him using borrowed money to pay off other borrowed money, and his working with Wall Street to ensure bonds were issued before the project was ever approved by regulators. In all those instances, millions were paid out in fees. His gleeful acknowledgment of that fact, in the face of the city's collapse, was more than telling.

"I really have to go now, I have a meeting in a few minutes." He turned his back and started walking away.

"Mayor Reed," I followed him up the steps—the camera still recording on my shoulder. The media followed closely behind. "Can I get your email or phone number?" The Mayor had relocated his work office, but few knew to where. Which I'm sure was not by mistake.

Reed stopped and approached me. He softly placed his hand on my arm and looked directly into my eyes. "I will get a hold of you." I'll be honest. He made me want to believe him.

The 63-year-old then reached into the breast pocket of his suit coat and pulled out my business card, which he held taunt between his index and middle fingers. Over the months, I had left many at his home. I was utterly shocked to see he kept one on his person. I was unsure what it meant.

"I have this," he smiled. "I will contact you soon and we can talk." He then returned the card to his coat pocket.

In that moment, an internet photographer began snapping what must have been 50 shots of the icon. The Mayor's face flashed with the snap of the camera's shutter.

With a childish grin, he cheerfully raised his voice. "Do you have enough photos, or would you like me to pose for some?" The dozen or so people in the hallway bellowed like old fraternity brothers.

"This brings back memories," he said again. "This was like every day."

This day could have been a reckoning for Reed. But his savvy nature and quick wit simply demonstrated the political skills that allowed for his 28-year death grip on Harrisburg. He turned on the charm when necessary, yet remained stern if needed. His calm delivery in openly discussing the complex and chaotic nature of the topic made him appear less villainous and culpable.

During my interview with Reed, he continually spoke of a business meeting he must attend. But only when we exhausted our questions concerning his administration, did he truly run out of time.

"I didn't start working in Harrisburg until nine months after you left office," I mentioned to Reed as he approached the exit. "Linda Thompson is the only Harrisburg Mayor I've known."

"On that note," he replied, "I'll bite my tongue and leave." Which he did.

I'm still waiting for that email or phone call he promised me.

It was dubbed the "Great Flood of 2011" by the media. In the background, take note of the submerged bridge. The road beneath the flood water is generally 30 feet above the creek it spans.

The first receiver David Unkovic soon after his nomination was approved. Notice the hopefulness in his stare.

Unkovic's last media interview before resigning. His cheerful and optimistic demeanor steadily changed as he educated himself on what really happened to Harrisburg.

Mayor Reed early in his political career - perfectly shaven and manicured.

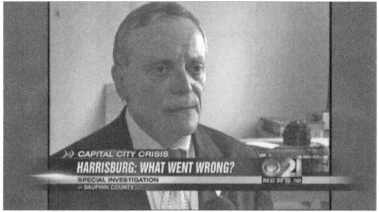

Stephen Reed, 28 years later after leaving office at age 60.

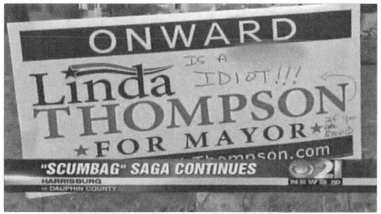

A vandalized campaign sign during the 2013 Mayoral Democratic Primary - perhaps courtesy a Perry County "Scumbag."

Mayor Thompson in mid-sentence of her "Scumbag" remark.

The second receiver retired Air Force Major General William Lynch. Here, he stands tall at his initial press conference following his nomination.

My early 20th century check stamp on my desk at CBS 21. Still functional after more than 100 years, it's a fine example of what America used to produce - while also symbolizing Mayor Reed's spending habits.

15: UNHEARD SCREAMS FOR JUSTICE

FOLLOWING THE SENATE HEARINGS on the incinerator, a ranking committee member informed me some of those who testified likely committed perjury. But no charges were ever filed. In fact, I never heard another thing about it, which didn't surprise me. This lack of accountability had become expected. Harrisburg had been murdered, but justice on her behalf—and that of the taxpayer—was never realized. But this absence of culpability was not due to a shortage of demand.

Before David Unkovic, the first receiver, resigned, he called for federal and state prosecutors to investigate Harrisburg's debt. Much of the evidence supporting his request was found in the forensic audit released by the Harrisburg Authority.

"I think [city residents] have been ill-used by their own government and by the many actors who were involved in the series of incinerator transactions," he said in despair hours before his departure.

Unkovic knew the bond deals were very risky and he couldn't discount the possibility of illegal activity in their ratification. I believe he knew those statements predicated the necessity of his stepping down. Many assumed he discovered too much. The man who replaced him made no similar calls for action.

But Unkovic was not unaided in his demands. He had gobs of support. "We as individuals made our calls," said Neil Grover of Debt Watch Harrisburg—a local advocacy group. "We have more than 170 members that have called state, federal and local prosecutors asking, 'Why won't you do something about this?'"

Harrisburg City Council's bankruptcy attorney, Mark Schwartz, sent requests for investigations to the IRS and SEC. He claimed the bonds secured by the city for the incinerator were not properly issued. And there was never an attempt or desire to pay them off.

"These bonds are a Ponzi Scheme," Schwartz told me in an interview after he filed the requests. "This was just a bond issue to help stave off the problem to get to the next bond issue. Where I'm concerned, this was a colossal rip off."

City Council wanted its own justice. This was my report on January 19th of 2012:

Anchor Intro:
Harrisburg City Council has unanimously approved a resolution asking the U.S. Department of Justice to investigate Harrisburg and find out exactly what led to the financial crisis. CBS 21's Chris Papst is live with the Dauphin County Mobile Newsroom in Harrisburg with more, Chris.

Papst Reporter Intro:
When the forensic audit on the incinerator came out last week, it did answer many questions but it also raised a lot more. And many of those questions revolve around former Mayor Stephen Reed.

Package Report:
He was Harrisburg's longest serving mayor and its most popular. But Stephen Reed's involvement in Harrisburg's

financial crisis has cast a cloud of doubt over his 28-year legacy. When the Harrisburg Authority released its much-anticipated forensic audit on the incinerator, it concluded that many people were at fault for this crisis, specifically Mayor Reed.

Brad Koplinski: City Council Member

"Everyone involved in this deal was concerned about closing the deal. This is all about bond issues and nobody gets paid unless the bond gets issued—unless the deal gets done."

And according to the audit, Mayor Reed was the man in charge of getting the deal done. The audit states:

Harrisburg Authority Incinerator Forensic Audit: 2012

"The decisions related to the retrofit and the related financial issues were directed by and vetted through the highest levels of leadership at the city, as Mayor Stephen Reed and his closest advisors... were prominently involved in the decision-making process."

In recent testimony, city attorney, Andy Giorgione, said Reed had "certain interpretations of what the law said, what needed to be submitted to Council and what didn't. I don't know what else to say than he signed documents if he felt he could bind the city. You didn't tell him to. He told you what to do."

If that's true, why did Mayor Reed decide to go forward with the project? The technology was unproven, the estimates were flimsy, at best, and the work was not insured. Many feel the answer lies in the documents that have yet to be turned over; hence the need for a federal investigation.

Brad Koplinski: City Council Member

"All of these things are very concerning and the only way to find out is to get federal subpoena power and a full investigation to get all the answers for taxpayers of Harrisburg and the region."

Papst Reporter Tag:

The resolution that Council passed last night will be sent to Attorney General Eric Holder at the Justice

Department early next week. More than 1000 signatures from Harrisburg residents requesting the investigation will be sent with it.

END SCRIPT

Shortly after that report, we did learn the Security and Exchange Commission was investigating Harrisburg. The scope and even the subject were uncertain. But I had confirmed the agency had subpoenaed documents from the city and the Authority. We also knew the city had spent $225,000 on legal fees. Many held high hopes this would amount to something substantial.

Though, an equal hope could not be found in the local District Attorney, Ed Marsico. He told me criminal charges involving incinerator bonds lay outside his jurisdiction limiting his ability to investigate.

Adding to the frustration surrounding this void of burden lay in the existence of proven nefarious behavior during the Reed years.

The Pennsylvania Ethics Commission fined Fred Clark $1,185 for taking a Blackberry and computer during his time with the Authority. When I questioned Clark about the allegations, he said he wrote a check for the missing amount. "I do well financially. I don't need to take stuff. I didn't even know I took it. This whole investigation is bullshit."

Clark served as Authority Chairman while simultaneously working as a consultant for Reynolds—a company that received incinerator retrofit contracts. This apparent conflict of interest was pointed out in the forensic audit. "We have seen no evidence that any of Reynold's contracts were competitively bid," it stated. Clark defended himself by citing his abstaining from Authority votes concerning Reynolds. Remember the office space near the river where Reed worked? That was Clark's. The audit points out Clark also contributed $22,781 to Reed's campaigns from 2000-2010. But Reynolds received at least $850,000 in incinerator fees.

James Ellison, another former chair of the Authority and school district counsel when Reed took it over, was also investigated for ethics violations. He had worked on Reed's re-election campaigns and was fined $2,297 for a conflict of interest relating to his time at the Authority. In early 2014, a neighboring District Attorney announced an investigation into Ellison for overcharging a school district as solicitor.

The audit also stated that Ellison and his law firm, Rhoads and Sinon, declined to provide certain requested documents. This also held true for Giorgione's law firm, Buchanon, Ingersoll & Rooney and the financial advisors Milt Lopus.

Though, giving what was already known, people were anxious, impatient and ready for revenge. But little appeared to be happening.

Before resigning, Unkovic said the incinerator debacle was the result of a joint venture between various parties. Each sought different means in the same goal. Stephen Reed, and the Authority, desired additional revenues. Dauphin County wished to part ways with its controversial landfill. And bond insurer, FSA, which already had $100 million tied up in the incinerator, simply wanted paid. All yearnings could be satisfied via the retrofit.

Here's a more detailed explanation of what happened and why many say those involved should be held criminally accountable.

The aforementioned forensic audit, stuffed with 460 footnotes and 8,000 pages of supporting data, was drafted by a team of accountants and fraud investigators who gathered information on the incinerator financing to analyze what went wrong. Some of the auditors worked for CPA firms, others law firms. It was released in January of 2012 and unequivocally stated the city's financial collapse was brought about by a failure to fully comply with state law. In other words, it was criminal.

The main players in the audit are Mayor Reed, The Harrisburg Authority, Dauphin County, City Council, FSA (now AGM, a municipal bond insurer), Barlow (the first contractor hired to perform the retrofit), Milt Lopus (financial advisors to the Authority) and IMAGE (SWAP advisor to the Authority). Remember, the "independent" Harrisburg Authority owned the incinerator, not the city.

Perhaps the most dubious aspect of the incinerator retrofit project lay in the certifications that declared the incinerator debt; self-liquidating—meaning future revenues from the project would pay for the debt incurred. At the time, Harrisburg was bound by state-imposed debt limits, which it had reached. Thus, Reed was barred from borrowing the money needed to update the facility. Unless, however, the debt was certified self-liquidating.

If the project gained that title, the bonds could legally be issued. If that title was not granted, the city was prohibited from accruing additional debt. The audit claims the eventual certifications were not rooted in reality. "[The lawyers and consultants] do not appear to have adequately identified or responded to numerous red flags that, if heeded, could have led to a different outcome," it said. "In some cases, the Authority, the city and the county took strained positions on state law regarding municipal debt financing and other issues to allow the retrofit and related financing to proceed."

These "red flags" were either ignored, or simply viewed as an obstacle that required added creativity. Mayor Stephen Reed and County Commissioner Jeff Haste eventually signed self-liquidating certifications. In doing so, the audit noted, "we have seen no evidence of what was discussed or how the issue was resolved."

It might not surprise you the lawyers and consultants for the retrofit financing came from very well-connected firms in Pennsylvania. It may also not surprise you the audit found it was common for these firms to have close ties to Mayor Reed or donate to his campaign.

In several instances, these lawyers and consultants got paid "significant fees". Eckert Seamans alone collected more than $3 million on the project, $634,500 of that were fees—according to the audit. And coincidentally, some of the self-liquidating debt certifications in 2007 were based upon the analysis of Eckert Seamans attorneys.

When these self-liquidating certifications were ultimately offered to the state, they weren't checked for accuracy. The Department of Community and Economic Development had precedent to object, but did not. A spokesman for DCED later told me the agency is not investigative in nature. The process is not designed to question the claims of local government officials—it just accepts the information as truth. Hence, the state took no responsibility.

The numbers below detail the shocking extent to which Barlow's projections for self-liquidation were incorrect. The figures compare the actual debt service versus what was estimated in the contractor's report.

Actual/Budgeted Income
Before Debt Service vs. Projections
(in millions)

Year	Actual/Budget	Projection	Variance
2006	($2.2)	$13.2	($15.4)
2007	(4.0)	13.7	(17.7)
2008	2.4	13.6	(11.2)
2009	2.1	14.1	(12.0)
2010	0.5	14.1	(13.6)
2011	5.6	13.7	(8.1)
Total	$4.4	$82.4	($78.0)

Not only were Barlow's estimates off by $78 million, the audit explains certain professional fees were not included. These fees involved legal, engineering, facilities management and audit services. They ranged from $1.4 million and $1.7 million annually between 2009 and 2011. Barlow's 2003 projections also did not include $3.8 million in Indenture Reserve that the incinerator incurred in 2010. Barlow's projections were off by an astounding $87 million, leading the authors of the audit to conclude:

"We have seen no documents showing that the Authority, the city, [county] or any of their advisors, performed a serious analysis.

"It appears that the Barlow financial projections may have been of less concern than normally would be expected because it was the city and county guarantees, as well as FSA's bond insurance, that seem to have been the means used to procure financing and sell the 2003 bonds, not the merits of the project."

The issue concerning self-liquidating debt was merely one blunder in the project. The audit explains how the deal itself was organized in a highly irresponsible way.

"Based upon our analysis of the projections, and the circumstances surrounding their development, the projections appear to have been highly dependent on assumptions that the retrofit would be completed on-time and on-budget, with virtually no margin for error. If certain assumptions are adjusted even slightly, the project would not be feasible. Because a reasonable cushion for debt service coverage was not built into the structure, the finance professionals, city, county and FSA left no margin for error.

"However, even if Barlow had completed the project on time, the significant deficiencies highlighted in the projections would have provided substantial challenges to the Authority's ability to service the debt."

During his senate hearing, Reed claimed no professional who analyzed the deal raised concerns over its projected financing. The audit refuted that and offered an explanation for why concern was overlooked.

"We have identified information where one of the professionals involved with the city and the Authority dismissed a financial analysis of the project as a tool for assessing the reasonableness of buying the 2003 bonds. In a December 18, 2003 email message, Mr. Losty of RBC (Royal Bank of Canada—underwriter for the deal) communicated with an individual from TRowePrice, stating, "My only word of advice is if you are trying to evaluate this on a revenue generating basis, you are the only one including the bond insurer. Bottom line is that there is an AA county with a full faith and credit general obligation pledge."

In another instance, the audit found more dissent.

"Even though due diligence [by City Council and the county] was performed, we have found no evidence that the consultants retained by either entity provided any meaningful challenge to the [project's] projections, even though one of those consultants, Buchart Horn, indicated that, in its estimation, the project would not be able to generate cash flow sufficient to service all of the debt.

"We have seen no indication [that] City Council, or any of the other parties involved in the decision to undertake the Barlow Retrofit, considered Buchart Horn's conclusion."

The audit continued:

"The reliance on the assumptions contained in the [contractor's] projections is difficult to understand given that the projections were presented to a number of professional firms that City Council and the county retained in connection with the 2003 retrofit debt issuance."

As mentioned, the contractor hired to perform the retrofit was Barlow Project Inc. The Colorado based company's patented burner technology was new, exciting and thoroughly untested. Barlow's ambitious mechanics utilized high-pressure blasts of air instead of mechanical grates to burn the trash. In theory, it was highly effective and far less expensive. In reality, it had never been done on a scale this large.

Barlow's original cost estimates were $50 million lower than its nearest competitor. And given the incinerator's existing $104 million in debt when the EPA shut it down, the offer was clearly enticing. Plus, Barlow's future depended on the project's success. He had motive to ensure results. It was the perfect storm. The audit says no evidence exists that any other contractor was seriously considered.

Yes, there were some concerns that Barlow could not deliver. But they were negated by Dauphin County's guarantee of the project. As noted in the audit, suddenly, the viability of the retrofit seemed less important. With the backing of 250,000 county taxpayers, everyone would surely get paid.

"This entire process has been about greed," Brad Koplinski, "gang of four" member, would later say. "No one got paid unless the deals went through. They said and did whatever it took to clear the deal and get the paychecks. In the end, they left the people of the city holding the bag."

As for the performance bond, Council members said they didn't know Barlow was ineligible due to poor financial condition. Then Council Member Linda Thompson said she would not have approved the project had she known. Harrisburg Authority members also claimed to be unaware. Ditto Reed.

Performance bonds serve as insurance policies and are legally required in Pennsylvania for any public project over $10,000. The first incinerator contract offered to the state did have a performance bond, according to the audit. The final one did not. The audit explains how the original contract contained the term "performance bond." But that term was crossed out, replaced in later contracts with "Surety Bond" or "equipment delivery, assembly and installation" bond. And these insurances covered but a small percentage of the project. Yet, the deal was still approved by state regulators.

The combination of no performance bond and dubious financial predictions convinced stakeholders the project was wrought with "substantial risk", which is why the city and county were forced to guarantee the debt. But not without first receiving millions in fees. However, the audit states when the city received those guarantee fees, the money was not used for the incinerator, but rather to help balance the city's budget, "further damaging the [incinerator's] ability to pay its operating expenses and debt service" while providing "little, if any, benefit to the retrofit project." The audit concluded, "It was clear that the city would not have the financial ability to pay on its guarantee, and that the county would have to provide credit backing, which essentially is what occurred."

The audit's explanation concerning Fred Clark's apparent conflict of interest as an Authority Board member and employee of Reynolds provided noteworthy insight into the mentality of those involved.

> "In June 2003, in response to Mr. Clark's expression to the Authority of Reynolds' interest in the project, Rhoads & Sinon, then legal counsel to the Authority, conducted a legal analysis regarding conflicts of interest. They concluded that no member of the Authority could have even an indirect interest in a contract with the Authority, and that doing so would violate the conflict of interest provisions in the Municipal Authorities Act (the "MAA"). The Rhoads & Sinon analysis further stated that any contract that was made in violation of the MAA would be void. Given the conclusion reached by Rhoads & Sinon, and our own analysis, Mr. Clark had a conflict of interest and Reynolds should not have been permitted to contract with the Authority."

Yet, that report appears to have been dismissed as Clark remained heavily involved.

And then there was this: When the debt to retrofit the incinerator was issued, it included multiple "swaps" and "caps" the audit deemed, "unnecessarily complex." Though, they "resulted in the payment of excessive fees" while increasing "risk and [adding to] the potential for greater financial burden on the Authority."

The audit not only questioned the need for these swaps and caps, but the legality of them.

The audit stated: "To enable the city and county to enter into all of the swaps under the Debt Act, PFM, Milt Lopus and IMAGE provided certifications stating that the financial terms and conditions of the swaps were 'fair and reasonable.' The basis for the certifications... does not appear in any of the documents we were provided, nor was it apparent from any of the interviews conducted. It is not clear that the swaps were fair and reasonable within the overall context of the Retrofit."

It continued: "In several instances, it seemed that these advisors allowed transactions to occur with very little analysis of the risk or potential cost. We saw no evidence that FSA questioned any of these transactions.

"From the documents reviewed, it does not appear that the financial advisors for the Authority or the county (Milt Lopus; PFM; IMAGE), provided significant guidance to the Authority, the city or the county consistent with managing interest rate risk or interest cost with respect to the use of all of these swaps and caps."

Most significantly, the audit stated, "We have seen no information suggesting that the Authority could not issue traditional floating rate debt." In other words, the swaps and caps were unnecessary. They provided no benefit to the project. But they did benefit the professionals, who collected millions in fees.

The audit added, "In several instances, it appears the professional advisors were encouraging the Authority to take actions aimed primarily at raising short-term funds irrespective of whether the transaction was prudent or risk was being increased. [For example,] we have seen no rationale at the time explaining why it would be reasonable for the Authority to spend $2 million (using debt proceeds) to purchase interest rate caps."

An interest rate cap is a type of swap where one party pays another if an interest rate exceeds an agreed upon amount. This is done in exchange for a fee, of course. Under normal conditions, caps are used to hedge against rising interest rates to protect the borrower.

Given the nature of the incinerator bonds, the auditors speculated on the true reason behind the swaps and caps: "It appears that the decision to enter into several of the transactions may have been driven primarily by the immediate need for money and may not have been permissible under the Debt Act."

Despite all the warnings and "red flags," the bonds were issued and Barlow was hired to start the project. Though, he never finished it. In 2006, Barlow Projects Inc. went bankrupt before the facility was completed. Meanwhile, the tens of millions that exchanged hands between all the swaps, caps and bonds, were gone. There was no funding to complete the work and no performance bond to fall back on.

In 2007, millions more were borrowed to hire a new company to finished the work. This new debt was also considered self-liquidating, which allowed for its issuance. Of course, the Auditors questioned the intent.

"While there are indications that analyses addressing the situation were conducted, it appears that the analyses were focused solely on taking on additional debt to complete construction, to provide working capital during the completion period, to reimburse the city and the county, and to pay professionals, rather than on whether the projections supported the [incinerator's] ability to satisfy the debt."

And that brings us to what many consider the real reason behind it all.

The numbers below presents the overall fees paid to those involved in the various incinerator financial deals, including swaps and caps. You may recognize many of these names. They may be involved in financial deals in your town.

PROFESSIONAL FEES

Barlow	$20,000
Bear Stearns & Co.	$118,942
Commerce Bank	$37,000
Dilworth Paxson	$50,000
Eckert Seamans	$634,500
Foreman & Foreman	$20,425
FSA (AGM: Assured Guaranty Municipal)	$3,083,779
HDR Engineering	$38,500
HRG Engineering	$245,500
J.P. Morgan Trust Company	$7,950
Klett Rooney Lieber & Schorling	$100,000
Mette, Evans, Woodside	$237,250
Milt Lopus Associates	$310,000
Obermayer, Rebmann, Maxwell & Hippel, LLP	$464,792
PFM	$177,410
Royal Bank of Canada	$5,922,878
Rhoads and Sinon, LLP	$25,000
Susquehanna Group Advisors	$115,000
Total Fees Paid to Professionals	**$11,649,862**

MUNICIPAL FEES

County	$1.9 million
City	$2.8 million
Total Fees Paid for Incinerator Financing	**$16,349,862**

As you can see, this project made many people and institutions millions. Yet, aside from those fees, the authors of the audit also question the necessity of many more millions paid out to professionals in work orders. While all this likely increased Reed's institutional popularity, the madness also signaled a newfound skepticism of his leadership and a reigning in of his power.

In 2006, Council, newly populated with Reed critics, challenged the "Mayor for Life." They passed a bill empowering the legislative branch, not the Mayor, to appoint Authority members. Naturally, Reed vetoed the measure. In a strong show of defiance, Reed's veto was overridden by Council.

For years, Reed had used the Authority as his personal piggy bank and he was unwilling to surrender control. At the Mayor's request an injunction was granted. The battle eventually reached the PA Supreme Court, where the Mayor won.

Coincidentally, it was the following election that the newly tested and therefore less-powerful Reed lost to Thompson—an election where he no longer seemed interested in the job.

Now, after all that has happened, everyone simply blames everyone else. City Council blames the Authority, Barlow, the Mayor, the county and the professionals. The Authority blames the professionals, Barlow, the Mayor, the county and City Council. The professionals blame Barlow, the Mayor, the county, City Council and the Authority. The Mayor blames the professionals, Barlow, the Authority, the county and Council. The county blames the professionals, Barlow, the Authority, City Council and the Mayor. I'm not sure whom Barlow blames.

"As the forensic audit released by the Harrisburg Authority showed, people in institutions in which this community placed its trust, failed to meet their obligations," Council member Koplinski told me. "Instead of doing what was right, they turned a blind eye to conflicts of interest. They allowed a plan to go forward they knew was not financially feasible."

So, that's how a town accumulates $350 million in debt on a facility worth a third that amount—in a city with a budget a seventh that amount. Is it possible that what happened was simply a lengthy series of honest missteps and miscalculations? Perhaps. I don't know. But what I do know is that nobody involved *wanted* this to happen—perhaps, similar to how Bernie Madoff didn't *want* to get caught.

Either way, armed with the information newly released from the audit, in addition to the near endless calls for investigations, I was able to file this story in July of 2012.

Afterwards, I received an email from David Unkovic that simply said, "Interesting."

Anchor Intro:

And now to our continuing coverage of the Capital City in Crisis. Only CBS 21 news has obtained startling information that is sending shock waves throughout Harrisburg and it centers on former Mayor Stephen Reed. CBS 21's Chris Papst is live with the Dauphin County Mobile Newsroom in Harrisburg with the details you will only see on CBS 21. Chris, you've been working on this story for months, tell us what you discovered.

Papst Reporter Intro:

Multiple sources have confirmed to me that a federal grand jury has convened in Williamsport to investigate Harrisburg's Financial Crisis, specifically, former Mayor Stephen Reed for public corruption. I have also been told the U.S. Justice Department is ramping up the investigation and bringing more agents to Harrisburg. And these agents won't be in the federal building. They'll be in a remote office so they can work in secret.

Package Report:

He was once one of Pennsylvania's most popular mayors—highly respected and admired. But now, sources tell CBS 21 news, the administration credited with saving and revitalizing Harrisburg is being investigated for public corruption.

When Mayor Stephen Reed took over Harrisburg in 1982 the city was in terrible financial shape. It's rumored the previous Mayor left bankruptcy papers on his desk. With few resources, Mayor Reed was able to turn the city around. But as soon as he left office after 28 years, it all came apart. With a debt seven times its annual budget, City Council has filed for bankruptcy; the state has taken over; and a receiver has been appointed. And many are wondering how this could have happened.

Sources tell CBS 21 news the Grand Jury is looking at evidence concerning campaign contributions and if former Harrisburg officials personally profited off city business. One piece of the federal investigation, we're told, includes a bank account from Pottsville that Reed funded with $7 million from the sale of water bonds. It's a story you saw a few months ago on CBS 21 news. This is a copy of the account. Reed opened it without the approval of City Council in the early 90s and much of the money went to people and businesses in the city. Sources also tell CBS 21 News that the investigation is looking into artifacts that Reed bought as mayor to see if anyone personally profited off them.

Over the months, we have tried numerous times to speak to Mayor Reed at his office and his home about this story. He has not made himself available for comment.

Reporter Outcue:
Sources also tell me the federal grand jury is looking at Dauphin County Commissioners and other former city employees to see if any laws were broken that led to this financial crisis.

Anchor Question:
Have you spoken to the U.S. Attorney who's leading the investigation?

Papst Answer:
I spoke to his office today and they told me no comment. Grand Juries are very secretive. The jury itself is told by the court not to talk. Lawyers for the witnesses, by law, cannot talk. And it's strongly suggested that the witnesses themselves, don't talk.
END SCRIPT

The day after this story aired, I was sitting at my desk and received a call from a blocked number. I thought it was my source. I was wrong.

"This is Chris," I answered.

"Chris Papst?" I did not recognize the raucous voice.

"Yes."

The man was not friendly, polite or patient. "This is Peter Smith." The U.S. Attorney for the Middle District of Pennsylvania. The man who assembled and was running the grand jury I had just exposed.

"I'm not sure who your sources are," he barked. "But they are wrong. You know how many calls I got about your story, last night?"

"Sir, I don't."

"I got plenty," he barely let me finished by reply. "I thought about sending out a press release correcting the record, but I didn't think it was that big of a deal."

Of course, my first thought was, "if it's not that big of a deal, why are you calling me?" But instead, I said, "I will revisit my sources, Mr. Smith," I wasn't willing to fight with the man. "But they told me they were in Williamsport and testified."

"I'm telling you, there is *no* grand jury and if you continue to report this, you do so at your own journalistic reputation."

"I called your office, yesterday." I wanted to know how far he was willing to go. "No one called me back or was willing to give me an answer."

For the first time in the conversation, he didn't jump over the end of my sentence. "I didn't get that call."

We shared a telling moment of silence.

"There is no grand jury." At this point, I knew the conversation was over. "I'd suggest you do more work and get the story right, next time." He then hung up.

When the phone went dead, I sat down in my chair and pondered what just happened. Yes, his words were strong. And his message stronger. But the simple fact that an agitated U.S. Attorney called me on my personal phone told me I was right.

As of the publishing of this book no indictments have come down from that Federal grand jury. It was also reported in mid-2014 that a state grand jury has assembled in Pittsburgh to review the city's financial dealings. That body has also not yielded indictments as of this book's publishing.

As for the SEC's investigation, in May of 2013, it announced that Harrisburg, under Reed, "misled" bond buyers and violated anti-fraud rules. The federal agency said Harrisburg continually provided false financial statements that created undue risk to bond investors. The SEC said these charges represent the first time a municipality has been accused of issuing misleading financial statements that were not included in securities disclosures. By Dec. 31, 2007, the city's bonds and bond guarantees for its agencies totaled about $500 million, many times its $61 million budget, the agency said.

Yet, despite the seriousness of this charge, the SEC imposed no financial or criminal penalty on the city or those individuals responsible. In fact, the federal agency credited current city officials for their cooperation and remedial actions. But the SEC did order the city to stop violating financial disclosure rules. Thank God!

16: THE PLAN

OT SINCE CITY COUNCIL FILED for bankruptcy had Harrisburg received as much attention as it did prior to the artifacts auction in late July 2013. As part of the pathway towards un-collapse, city leaders embraced the selling of artifacts Stephen Reed had spent the better part of 28 years acquiring. Using the fees from his financial artistry, the "Mayor for Life" assembled one of the nation's finest historical compilations. Though, the time had now come to part ways.

Over the years, I had heard rumors of its grandeur. People spoke of the collection with awe. I figured, in all reality, it was moderately impressive. I likened the fables to northern fishing trips of long past—the kind where one's trophy musky gets bigger with the years. It was only when I witnessed the auction in person, that I realized those legends actually underestimated Reed's real accomplishments.

The auction was held on City Island under a large pavilion next to the Harrisburg Senator's baseball stadium. It was a great location for such a spectacle. Not only did it provide stunning vistas of the city's reflection in the river, but it also gave your eye and mind a true appreciation of what Mayor Reed achieved. The city skyline and everything on City Island, which included two stadiums, train rides, batting cages, miniature golf and more, were created by Reed. But now, what could have been his greatest achievement left unrealized was being sold off.

When I arrived at the auction to cover it for that evening's newscast, I was honestly amazed. Most of the big ticket items had been won. But much remained, as it waited to be claimed or shipped. Furniture, weapons, firearms, posters, trinkets—the degree to which he shopped was fantastic. I walked up and down the many rows examining it all. Hundreds of years of history lay before me—most of it in excellent shape. You couldn't help but question how one man could purchase all this over decades. And much of it was bought with city money accompanied by little notice or scorn. If anything exemplified his ability to act without reprisal, this was it.

"Hey, Chris." Mayor Thompson's spokesman approached me with an extended hand. "This is pretty amazing, isn't it?"

I nodded as I inspected an Indian headdress that appeared quite delicate. "I can't get over all this," I replied. "I'll be honest. I didn't think this collection would look like this."

"This will make the city millions that it desperately needs," he raised an eyebrow. "Did you bid on anything? You could contribute to the city's recovery."

"Bid?" I hadn't even considered it. Ever since I started in journalism, I shied away from story involvement. Some reporters relish the opportunity to include themselves in their reportage. That was never for me. My focus always lay in the subject and its subjects.

"You should buy something," he suggested. "Other media has. There's still plenty of stuff left. Get a little memento to remind yourself of your Harrisburg days."

His argument made sense. This auction represented an opportunity to own a tangible aspect of my career. I quickly remembered back to my days in Wyoming when I missed an opportunity to own a dinosaur bone from an excavation story. I always regretted that. I decided I would not regret this. Minutes later, I had my auction card and a seat in the front row.

Most of the items on the block at first weren't terribly interesting, and quite expensive. As much as I wanted something neat, I didn't want something pricey. Had I gone home that evening with an expensive purchase, I feared my wife would lack the appropriate understanding. So, I impatiently waited for something reasonably affordable.

Thankfully, it only took a few minutes before an item caught my interest. Standing before me, the auctioneer elevated a box stuffed with picture frames, hand tooled leather items and string jewelry. Basically, it was a box of junk. But it was a lot of junk. I figured there had to be something in there I would want.

The bid started at $20. Some guy immediately took it to $30. I hung in strong through the $30s and got it for $40. When it was delivered to my seat, I realized my assumption was wrong. It was truly a box full of junk containing nothing of interest.

I was now the disappointed owner of some Wild West themed frames cased in leather, two frames that resembled a corner store that lit up via batteries, and some hand tooled leather carrying cases. The items were clearly of high quality. But I had a strong feeling none of it would end up in my home. I needed something else. But with $40 bucks gone, it had to be cheap.

Sitting in my seat, I remembered arriving at the auction and immediately spotting an item I really liked. It perfectly signified the moment and epitomized my time in the city. I had no idea what it was worth, but I wanted it. I set a price in my head and waited for it to cross the block. Though, this auction was so big, I wasn't too worried if I didn't win it.

The sale had been massively promoted by hired auctioneer, Guernsey's, out of New York City, which divided the event into seven days. Here is a breakdown of the week followed by a more detailed list of what was available.

Day 1 - July 15 - 7AM (PT)
Mercantile, Country Store, Advertising, Primitives, Advertising, Lamps & Lighting, Vintage Clothing
African Artifacts

Day 2 - July 16 - 7AM (PT)
Important Spanish Colonial Artifacts,
Revolutionary War, War of 1812,
Civil War, Battle of Little Big Horn, Indian Wars, Maps.
The Presidents. Historical Documents and Books.

Day 3 - July 17 - 7AM (PT)
Antique Firearms
American Indian

Day 4 - July 18 - 7AM (PT)
American Indian

Day 5 - July 19 - 7AM (PT)
Wild West

Day 6 - July 20 - 7AM (PT)
Wild West

Day 7 - July 21 - 7AM (PT)
(No Online Bidding)
Variety of Items
Unstructured Day

★ **FIREARMS 500 Historic guns incl:**
Springfield • Winchester • Smith & Wesson • Remington • Colt
Pruitt Bros. • St. Louis • James Brown & Sons • Hopkins & Allen

★ **MILITARY & MARITIME**
Revolutionary to World War II (Gen. Patton)
Important Swords • Telescopes • Binnacles • Compasses
Anchors • Sextants

★ **HISTORIC WESTERN FIGURES**
Wyatt Earp • Jesse James • Buffalo Bill • Wild Bill Hickok
Doc Holliday • Annie Oakley

★ **SPANISH / MESICAN**
Early Colonial Artifacts & Pottery • Tularosa • Mesa Verde
Socorro • Pinto • St. John's Anasazi • Jeddito • Puerco

★ **AMERICAN INDIAN**
Sioux • Cheyenne • Apache • Northern Plains • Blackfoot
Navajo • Commanche

★ **AFRICAN AMERICAN**
& African Artifacts

★ **PRESIDENTIAL ARTIFACTS**
Teddy Roosevelt's Rifle • Lyndon Johnson's Stetson, etc.

★ **MERCANTILE**
Hundreds of Country Store Rarities Advertising • Signage

★ **WELLS FARGO**
Massive Collection

★ **EARLY WARS**
Revolutionary • Civil • Indian Wars

★ **IMPORTANT EPHEMERA**
Maps • Early Photographs • Posters

★ **LITTLE BIG HORN**
Historic Artifacts • Rare Tomahawks

★ **FURNITURE**
Western Saloons • Hotels • Brothels

★ **GAMBLING DEVICES**
Saloons • Hotels • Brothels

★ **ARTWORK**
Western Bronzes • Painting

★ **WAGONS**
Coaches • Carts

★ **RARE BOOKS & DOCUMENTS**

Guernsey's website explained:

"Early in our Nation's history... pioneers considered Harrisburg, Pennsylvania to be the 'Gateway to the West.' Years ago, the then Mayor of the Pennsylvania state capital saw the wisdom in creating a museum paying homage to those pioneering days. To create the magnificent institution he envisioned, the city spent millions for the acquisition of rare artifacts pertaining to the Old West. In the process, the Mayor also saw fit to assemble collections relating to the Revolutionary, Civil and Indian Wars, and a wide range of other historic collectibles.

"For various reasons, the Old West museum that the Mayor dreamt of was never built. The staggering collection he amassed on behalf of the city—consisting of more than 8,000 antiques, artifacts, firearms, and rare documents— has languished in Harrisburg's storage facilities. Now, in what is certain to be a massive and glorious event to be held in Harrisburg."

Although it's out of my character considering how the items were purchased, I didn't want to see the city sell this collection. Reed had spent countless hours and millions more on the artifacts than the city would reap in return. I wanted to see the city build the museums. Reed had bought the artifacts to build three: a Wild West Museum, African American History and Sports Hall of Fame. None of these highly ambitious visions were realized except the National Civil War Museum. But it could still have been. Reed's vision of a destination city was still possible.

But, in reality the funds were lacking and the optics were impossible. How could the city ask its creditors for concessions if it didn't sacrifice itself? But, all the hard work of collecting the artifacts was done. Now, money just needed to be raised for a place to house them. And theoretically, those museums would be additional revenue streams.

But I got the feeling most residents just wanted the Reed years to be over. People needed to move on. Though, their opinions really didn't matter. The receiver wanted the collection sold off. It was all part of "the plan."

"The plan" refers to the financial recovery map for the city. Everyone called it "the plan." City Council called it "the plan." Mayor Thompson called it "the plan." The receiver called it, "the plan." Every time I heard "the plan," I envisioned some old, creepy man sitting in a musty office slow-rolling his fingers slightly below his chin.

After David Unkovic resigned, Governor Corbett appointed—errr, I mean, nominated—a retired air force general to replace him. Corbett was unwilling to repeat his initial mistake, so he hired a military man accustomed to simply following orders. But much like Unkovic, William Lynch had a questionable past concerning conflicts of interest. When Lynch was head of the PA National Guard, he was highly criticized for acquiring land in northern PA for tank practice. That contract was scuttled but not without the land owners keeping $325,000 of a state deposit.

That land owner then became a donor of the Republican Party and was subsequently brought into Governor Corbett's cabinet as Secretary of Community and Economic Development, the very department overseeing Harrisburg's restructuring. The Secretary, Alan Walker, whose family company happily took the taxpayer money during the botched land deal, said he had no contact with Lynch during that 1999 property transaction. But now they had to work together to save Harrisburg. This conflict of interest didn't receive the attention it deserved when Lynch was nominated. Such a degree of fatigue had set in, few had the energy to care.

Lynch proved very different from Unkovic. He kept to himself. He did not run the gauntlet of town hall meetings, nor did he seem interested in befriending city residents or placating the media. He strictly focused on his orders—to unscrew Harrisburg with minimal political fallout.

I first met Lynch at one of his few public appearances soon after being nominated. It was early autumn and he teamed up with Mayor Thompson to deliver the State of the City address at the Hilton Harrisburg. During the question and answer session, the city's new receiver was asked how he'd know when the city was offered a good deal. He said in the straightest face possible to a few hundred of the region's most successful business people, "It's like porn, I'll know it when I see it."

The room wasn't sure how to react. But I laughed out loud. This guy was no non-sense and clearly not concerned with political correctness. I found it refreshing.

Though apparently, he wasn't in a hurry to acknowledge the sight of porn. It wasn't until August 26 of 2013 —nearly a year-and-a-half after Lynch was appointed— that "the plan" was submitted for court approval. This marked nearly three years after Mayor Thompson first requested Act 47 status. And nearly two years after Council filed for bankruptcy and the first receiver was appointed.

As with most political rhetoric, "the plan" was given a catchy name, "The Harrisburg Strong Plan." How could something with a name like that not be a success?

The 350-page scheme started with the sentence, "Harrisburg deserves a bright future." It continued to say, "The Strong Plan, if anything, illustrates how cooperation and leadership in a challenging environment can lead to workable solutions." It provides "a comprehensive set of initiatives and funding to allow the City of Harrisburg to address the myriad of financial challenges that have for many years plagued the city and impeded its growth."

The plan set about not just to solve the debt crisis and balance city budgets, it also created a new attitude and instilled a fresh operational system for the city. It wasn't just a recovery plan; it was a quasi-Constitution.

In the most basic terms, the plan purports to eliminate the incinerator debt, balance the budget through 2016 by shifting existing revenues, and put in place a system where Harrisburg can thrive without being financially gutted. To call it ambitious is quite the understatement.

Under "The Strong Plan," the incinerator was to be sold to the Lancaster County Solid Waste Management Authority, or LCSWMA, for around $125 million. At this point, the facility had $363 million in debt. So, clearly not enough. To cover the rest, Harrisburg would lease its parking garages, lots and metered parking spaces for 40 years to a public-private partnership for about $260 million. City debtors combined to offer about $100 million in concessions. But, in return, a profit sharing system through the parking garages was established with some other small funding means.

By the way, do the basics of the plan sound familiar? Sell the incinerator, long term lease the parking garages and get concessions from the creditors via perhaps a "tender offer" to close the remaining hole?

Moving on, city unions agreed to $4 million in concessions as the state promised $5 million in annual public safety subsidies (to which future assemblies are not bound). The General Obligation Debt was restructured. The earned income tax will remain at the elevated 2 percent through at least 2016. But there were no initial real estate tax increases.

To ensure the city has enough money, revenue streams were brokered with the new operator of the parking garages. Some other revenues are possible, but not certain. Millions were made available for economic development, infrastructure improvements, and legacy obligations. The plan also transfers the city's water and sewer ownership to the Harrisburg Authority, whose books are freshly anew.

The most interesting aspect of "The Strong Plan" may lay in the establishment of two independent non-profit organizations commissioned to help lead the city. The nine-member boards would not be elected by the people, but rather approved by the receiver. One 501c(3), the Harrisburg Strong Infrastructure Investment Corporation, will focus on roads, water and sewer lines. The other, the Harrisburg Strong Economic Development Corporation, will encourage job growth and investment in the city to grow the tax base. Another trust and board would be established to handle "other post-employment benefits" or OPEBs. Remember them? These non-profits are designed to decentralize decisions normally reserved for those elected to represent the people.

With this plan, bankruptcy is no longer Harrisburg's headline. But if it fails, Chapter 9 will certainly be its fate. No judge in the nation, at that point, could say Harrisburg didn't try. With the leasing or selling of its main assets and revenue streams, this will either be a great success or a grave disaster. Harrisburg now lacks the substance to allow for any other outcome.

On the outset, it appeared "The Strong Plan" addressed most everyone's concerns, even those who screamed for justice. "The Strong Plan" stated:

> "As is apparent to anyone reading the Forensic Report, the fundamental proposition that the Incinerator could realistically have 'paid for itself' from its net operating revenues appears to have been ill-conceived from the outset. The public expects that there be a means to obtain redress for these ill-fated decisions if there is evidence to support the allegation that highly imprudent actions were taken by those charged with protecting the city and its taxpayers against these very types of circumstances. The current receiver agrees with the public that these matters merit full consideration. The receiver intends to consider using every measure available, including litigation, to seek redress from those professionals and entities alleged to be responsible for the various decisions to proceed with the Incinerator retrofit project."

"The Harrisburg Strong Plan" was designed to be a beacon of hope for financially distressed municipalities throughout America. If it works, it could be sold as a road map to salvation. Or, will its success simply instill a moral hazard where elected leaders become more willing to engage in financial risk, knowing creditors and higher elected officials will offer leniency to stave off political liability?

Either way, after the plan was announced the obligatory statements abound:

Governor Tom Corbett: "I am proud of the work that has been done by the Office of the Receiver, along with the commitment of all the stakeholders involved in Harrisburg's recovery effort, to finding a viable solution to this extremely challenging problem. We believe this recovery plan will not only address Harrisburg's past financial difficulties and substantial debt, but also open the door for future growth, development and financial stability."

Harrisburg City Council: "Today, after years of fighting for a fair and justifiable solution for the citizens of Harrisburg, our city takes a giant step forward. In many ways, the proposed plan accomplishes the many things we have fought so hard for, such as: shared pain and responsibility; a debt solution that brings all major stakeholders to the table; and most importantly, a plan to realistically deal with Harrisburg's chronic structural deficit. City Council has stood firm on various issues and fought for a fair solution for our city—one where taxpayers would not be alone in shouldering the enormous cost of past mistakes. Now as we work together with our stakeholders to move Harrisburg past this fiscal crisis, we will continue to work diligently for the betterment of the citizens of Harrisburg, as is our duty, entrusted upon us taking the oath of office during these challenging and troubling times."

Receiver William Lynch: "With the support of the Governor's Office and the Commonwealth, we have been able to find unique solutions that may have not otherwise existed. There are many people who helped bring these solutions to the table and they all deserve a great deal of credit for their efforts. Harrisburg will have the tools to craft a stable financial future and the incinerator issue goes away. The next four or five years will be OK. But it's how the city uses the tools we have provided that will be a challenge. We want the city to be back in charge of its finances as soon as possible."

County Commissioners: "This is a historic day. We have resolved the single greatest financial crisis in our region's history. This recovery will usher in a new era of economic prosperity and growth in the city, which is getting a fresh start. We can now focus on redevelopment of our urban core. Working together, we protected taxpayers and ratepayers from unfair tax increases."

But it was Mayor Linda Thompson who, as expected, delivered the line that would lead the newscast that evening. "I thank God for watching over this great, beautiful city and using my leadership to get the job done." I watched her make that statement while in her Sunday best with decorative metal earrings pulling hard on her ears. She stood tall behind a podium in city hall proudly proclaiming, "If I had not stayed the course and placed [the city] under Act 47, who knows where we'd be today. You elected me to correct a situation that plagued the city for years. I'm humbled to come before you today and say thank you for allowing me to get the job done for the future of your city. I thank everyone involved for moving mountains."

The only real public opposition to the plan came from the city's Controller, Dan Miller (yes, the homosexual, evil little one). "I have very serious concerns with all of this," he told me. "I think their numbers are not correct. I think they made incorrect assumptions. There are potential expenses that are very important that were omitted. Our numbers show there are some big deficits looming. Time will tell. But we won't know until it's too late if we make a mistake today."

Shortly after the plan was released, Miller presented his findings of the plan to City Council. In all of the city's elected ranks, he was the only financial expert. A trained Certified Public Accountant, Miller had a successful and respected practice in the city. He tirelessly purported that bankruptcy was the city's best option for future stability. Following the plan's release, his calls grew louder and more urgent.

His presentation to Council was titled, "The poor pay more." Miller argued, the creditors and county—in comparison—made far fewer sacrifices than city residents. He implored Council to fight for a better deal that less serves the interest of the money lenders.

"We are trading democratic rights for a few pieces of silver," he stated. "This is a plan OF, BY and FOR the creditors. Harrisburg had no advocates in this plan."

When Council filed for bankruptcy, Miller pointed out that lobbyists, the county, and bond insurers led the charge in its ultimate rejection. Under Chapter 9, with a judge in control, those entities would likely have taken a more significant financial hit. He said they wanted control of the process to sway the end result in their favor, which they got outside of a bankruptcy court. Now, the taxpayer is receiving the brunt of the burden. Bankruptcy, he argued, would have protected the city's people and its assets. Instead, the plan gave both away.

"We'll be dead before this plan has run its course," he implored of "The Strong Plan's" 40-year outlook. "The city is giving its power to control rates, fees, parking enforcement, water, trash and recycling to people outside the city. The debt is not paid off, it's just shifted around."

He claimed after investigating the numbers that Harrisburg was still faced with $470 million in debt. "In the big picture the debt has not been reduced. What happens after 2016 when the receiver's plan for balanced budgets expires?"

"What we have here is a loss of self-government to these non-profits and trusts that the city won't control. This plan is saying, 'we don't trust the city to make decisions. We don't trust the citizens of Harrisburg to govern themselves.'" Miller delivered his message with energy and conviction before a crowded Council chamber. "Why are the [non-profits and trusts] being set up? So

Wall Street benefits from our lack of self-government. So the money goes to bond insurers. The money comes from city cash streams, but the city won't control it."

"These are basic functions of city government, infrastructure and economic development," Miller continued. "When the Mayor and Council want to do something, will we have to get the economic development corporation to agree with us? When it's all said and done and we look back on this, I have a feeling we are going to see city residents paying higher income tax, higher real estate tax, higher sewer and water rates, higher parking fees and fines." Miller contended bankruptcy would correct all this, minus the inevitable pain and negative stigma. "We can see the future coming. This is not a good plan for the city."

In the immediate aftermath of the plan's implementation, Miller—in part—was right. Parking rates, fees and fines skyrocketed. The new renters of the parking garages paid a ton of money and they sought to make that money back. Miller's passion, however, was encumbered by a lost will to fight. Council and the Mayor were tired. The receiver's vision would be approved.

This "Strong Plan" came just one month after the artifacts auction, which did offer the city a better financial position. Ten thousand people participated online and hundreds more bid in person. Despite the lack of documents authenticating many of the items, the 8,000 artifacts sold for $3.85 million. Of that, the city collected $2.7 million, which it used to pay debt. Two other smaller auctions sold an additional 2,000 pieces for $1.6 million.

It's unclear how much Reed spent for the items since there were no receipts or invoices for much of it. But most estimates seemed to hover around $8 million. A document signed by Wyatt and Mattie Earp fetched $55,000. That shared the high bid with Doc Holliday's frock coat. The gun slinger's dental chair went for $40,000. The totals were far beyond the estimates.

Reed himself never attended the auction. He told the local paper he bid on a few items through a friend, including an Army Scout jacket and a cowboy hat. He didn't win either.

As for me, a few minutes after I bought that box of junk, the item I really wanted came up. The bidding started at $20. Some guy quickly jumped on it. I offered $25, which he didn't challenge. That afternoon, I returned to the station with a turn-of-the-century check stamper. Purchased by Stephen Reed, made in America and heavy as hell, I thought it was fully appropriate. Forever, it will sit on my work desk as a reminder of what I spent years covering.

17: A NEW DAY

FOR MANY, MAY 21, 2013, was a circled date. The implementation of "The Strong Plan" had long been underway and the city was slowly healing. By year's end, the incinerator would be gone along with Harrisburg's crippling debt. The only remaining task to secure a more stable future was to fire the Mayor.

In a city like Harrisburg, the Democratic primary is the only contest that matters. General elections are irrelevant. The town had not elected a Republican to any position in decades. Its last GOP mayor was sworn in when the Oval Office was occupied by a peanut farmer. Along with other cities, like Detroit, Pennsylvania's capital is a case study in the consequences of one-party rule.

All the dubious "firsts" Harrisburg had achieved in the previous four years made this particular referendum an attractive one. And its importance was not lost upon city residents and anyone else watching. Campaign spending easily doubled the $275,000 dished out during the previous mayoral cycle. But most of the money did not go to the favorite. Early in the campaign, Controller Dan Miller appeared to have the upper hand. But a late infusion of cash turned bookstore owner Eric Papenfuse into the frontrunner. On Election Day, 6,600 ballots were cast as opposed to just 5,100 in the 2009 Democratic primary. It was nice to see a few more people caring.

Papenfuse was a local business owner, who built the Midtown Scholar Bookstore into one of the region's most popular and respected. In 2007, under Reed, he had briefly served on the Harrisburg Authority Board before resigning, citing a preponderance of fraud. This led to criticism of him being a "quitter." He argued he couldn't morally function amongst such dysfunction.

The messaging between the main candidates was simple. Papenfuse supported "The Strong Plan," while Miller favored bankruptcy. Unlike other elections, this truly was a referendum on the city's future.

Thompson tried to stay relevant, but any hope she had of a second term died with her "scumbags" statement. The fourth candidate, Lewis Butts, simply supplied comic relief. To this day, his glib explanation to me on camera, "I spray-painted p-u-s-s on Papenfuse to make it, Papen-puss," following charges he vandalized his rival's campaign signs the day before the election, is the single greatest sound bite of my career—a title that will likely endure. For that, I thank him.

The day following that doozie, with Butts still wondering how he got caught, I was assigned to cover Thompson's campaign.

"Why are you putting me with Thompson?" I asked management with revulsion. "You know she loathes me. After three-and-a-half years she still refers to me as 'you,'" I explained. "And it's not a very friendly, 'you'."

My argument persuaded no one.

Thompson held her party in the strangest of locations, the National Civil War Museum. The strange aspect did not lie in the actual location—the museum has beautiful banquet rooms—but rather in its symbolism. This was the house that Reed built and she was destined to lose. Although, looking back, it seems fitting she would perform one final head-scratching act.

As we waited for the returns, the room was set with shadowed lighting and baby-making smooth jazz. Fried chicken and Heineken soothed her paid staffers unsettled nerves. The relatively small room never got more than a quarter full. Thompson hadn't raised much money. And at $100 a staffer, her funds quickly depleted. I didn't notice any unpaid support, or white people (besides the media, that is) in the entire place.

Thompson's election was indeed historic. But everyone knew it was coming to an end. And the mood of the room wholly reflection that realism. Over the course of her administration, Thompson endlessly bragged of her status as the first female and first African American to lead Harrisburg. It was certainly a title she earned—one that cannot be taken away. But this night would render her primary accomplishment past tense.

Four years earlier, when Thompson beat Reed in the Democratic Primary, most everyone was shocked. I wasn't working in the city yet, but I would assume those aghast included Thompson, herself. I heard many a rationale for why Reed lost. Some claimed Thompson simply rode the Obama wave of black voter registration and enthusiasm. I heard a few people blame the loss on the rain that had besieged primary night. Perhaps it kept many voters home who were less enthusiastic and just assumed Reed would win an eighth term as easily as he won the first seven. This reasoning would seem logical but for the fact that it didn't rain.

Thompson beat Reed by 1,000 votes that night. And went on to beat her Republican challenger by 800. Many Democrats boldly crossed over and voted for the GOP candidate. But not enough.

After Thompson won the primary, she held a two-hour ceremony and swearing in. It was reported that 1000 people watched her take the oath in a large city audi-torium. Amongst a ceremony of prayers, ministers and gospel hymns, Thompson eventually took to the podium to declare with heavenly re-verb, "To God be the glory." In a gray suit-skirt with a giant flower thing on her lapel, she spoke in the tone of a Baptist minister. "To God be the glory. I have to say that because I am absolutely nothing without him. I can't breathe without him. I have no wisdom without him. And I certainly can't love all of you without him."

Her 20-minute speech focused on the need for solidarity.

"My prayer is for our city to come together, united in a common purpose, finding strength in our unity."

She discussed the need to not criticize, but to encourage. "With neither malice or blame that has no place in civil discourse, but with love for our city and all our fellow citizens, we must join hands in recognition of our collective future."

With that said, she then began to criticize.

"Past administration policy now threaten the city's ability to provide basic public services. We cannot allow this to happen. Poor financial management and excessive spending in the past will require us to take drastic measures. City operations are already understaffed. Previous administrations have attempted to solve 21st century financial problems with 20th century technology and 19th century techniques. Our city's finances are in great disrepair. We have inherited numerous challenges—significant and daunting."

Harrisburg's new mayor then took command.

"Make no mistake, I will make the tough decision necessary to secure our financial stability and protect future generations from harm. Saving our city starts here and it starts today. It starts with you and it starts with me. I cannot rescue a city alone."

She then channeled her political hero, a man whose face and image would decorate nearly every wall of her mayoral suite, President Barack Obama.

"Real change has not come to Harrisburg yet, but mark my words, real change begins today. Marching together we win the victory. Let us go to work. God bless this city and this great nation." With a princess wave not to be seen again until spurred by a snowball, she admired her standing ovation.

That night, hundreds of people paid $100 a ticket to sell out Thompson's inaugural ball at the historic Farm Show Complex. It was a decadent night brimming with tuxedos, jeweled attire, live Jazz, and VIP rooms. Thompson graced the evening in a Victorian style, taupe gown with few accessories other than a giant smile. Her grand entrance came accompanied by a rendition of Frank Sinatra's "I've got the world on a string" (PennLive).

Dinner guests dined on a menu of Asian cuisine and barbecue. New arrivals were welcomed by a harp player and ballerinas. The local paper reported a price tag of $60,000. That included the table reserved by Eckert Seamans (PennLive).

This party seemed to lack congruence with the speech Thompson had delivered just hours earlier. A speech in which she lamented a city in "financial disrepair" and declared "My prayer is for our city to come together." I guess her calls for unity only applied to those with substantial disposable income.

"Of each of us, much will be asked," Thompson affirmed in her inaugural address. "Of each of us, much will be sacrificed." Clearly.

Back to the primary election of 2013—It wasn't until after 10pm that a tired and defeated Linda Thompson entered her campaign headquarters in the Civil War Museum. There was no pomp, no circumstance, no harp players. She simply greeted a few of her staffers and delivered a hoarse concession speech.

"Hi, everybody." Her tone lacked its usual acridity. "It was an honor to have been mayor of this city. The voters have spoken that they are looking for change. And I accept that with much humbleness. It really is about the will of the people and I will make sure the transition is done smoothly."

It had certainly been a rough four years.

"I was raised by the people. Education by the people. And certainly got my morals and values here." As she addressed her small group of supporters, she seemed real. Her voice never piqued with its customary spite and tenacity. She was talking *to* the people, not *at* them. This was the real Linda Thompson and I liked it.

"I certainly hold that as a sacred trust," she smiled genuinely, something I also had rarely, if ever, seen. "I don't find this as a failure because I did the people's work over the past three-and-a-half years. So I go out with my head high and not hanging low and know that God's on the throne and that there are better days ahead."

After the speech, Thompson gave live interviews in the 10:00 and at 11:00 p.m. newscasts with reporters from other stations, but not me. I was left to synopsize her campaign and run a sound bite from her concession speech. My managers weren't too happy to see the Mayor on our competitor's air. But hell, I told them that would happen.

The enthusiasm over Papenfuse's win wasn't as much generated by his victory as it was Thompson's defeat. Social media exploded that evening with harsh comments of farewell.

And the embarrassing manner in which Thompson lost incited further criticism. In a city that's 75 percent minority, she placed a distant third to two white guys.

> Eric Papenfuse: 2480
> Dan Miller: 2084
> Thompson: 1816
> Lewis Butts: 84

Many had worried the end game became jeopardized when Papenfuse entered the race against Miller—thus splitting the white vote. Most assumed the majority of blacks would stay loyal to Thompson. They didn't.

That night in the Civil War Museum, I watched closely as the Mayor greeted her staffers following her concession speech. She never worked the room as the spitfire Mayor who had something to prove. She was just Linda.

Despite our strained relationship, I felt bad for her. Her intentions were always good. But I feel she became too consumed with her own historical significance and refused to allow others an opportunity to usurp it—thus, making enemies. However, notwithstanding all her ridiculousness and buffoonery, her administration was indeed a success. All we can ask of our elected leaders is to leave our government in better shape than they found it. I can say unequivocally, Thompson did. Had Reed?

On the night of his primary victory, Eric Papenfuse promptly heralded a "new day." With this election, after 32 years, the last remnants of Reed's influence was gone (Thompson was originally elected to City Council as a member of The Reed Team. She later defected). The hierarchy of city government was now void of anyone connected to the "Mayor for Life."

To use a cliché, May 21, 2013 marked the end of an era; an era that saw incredible achievements and corresponding failures; an era that witnessed the making of a dictator and the plundering of his successor; an era of American history we must not dismiss as aberrant, but rather reject as a new norm.

But considering the circumstance, this question abounds: Does any of it really matter? The state is in control and the power of the people's vote has been negated. The bookstore Mayor's hands were tied. "The Strong Plan" left him in control of fewer assets and in less control of city funds. The plan's harshest critics likened Harrisburg's mayor to a puppet with fewer strings.

To his credit, that didn't seem to bother Papenfuse. Between the primary and inauguration, he remained infectiously positive.

"No one individual can do this job," he would say. "It's going to require tremendous amounts of support. It's going to require support from those who voted for my opponents. It's going to require assembling a whole new staff of individuals to work for the City of Harrisburg. We have openings galore and we're going to need to work very hard to fill them with the best and the brightest."

Papenfuse's demeanor is that of an ardent optimist. With wide eyes and flamboyant gestures, he fondly promoted the city he loves.

"Harrisburg's best days are yet to come," he continually repeated before his inauguration. A bold statement, considering how high the bar was set during the City Beautiful Movement. "With your help we are on our way to better schools, safer streets and a city that will be the envy of a nation.

"I want to thank the people of Harrisburg who have placed their trust in me to lead this city to a new era of pride and prosperity. Together, we can."

Before officially taking office, Papenfuse worked to mend relations with the suburbs and surrounding counties. He did the same with City Council by moving their offices from the dingy basement to less-stuffy fourth floor units. He also mended relations with the media. He even refers to me by name.

"I wish him well in moving Harrisburg forward," said City Controller Dan Miller, the man Papenfuse beat to become mayor. "Other than that, I want to paraphrase one of the great elected officials of America: He's in, I'm out, we'll see who's happier."

In January of 2014, Eric Papenfuse was sworn in as Harrisburg's 38th mayor. There was no grand ceremony, no extravagant inaugural ball, no live band, tuxedos or catered buffet. There wasn't even a speech.

"This is not a day for speeches," Papenfuse said on the day he took the oath. "It's a day for rolling up our sleeves."

Papenfuse held his inauguration in city hall at a cost of nearly nothing. Especially since he removed the police officer and metal detector Thompson had installed at the main entrance. About 200 onlookers simply walked in to witness the 20-minute ceremony that featured his swearing in along with four new Council members.

Papenfuse's address to the city was limited to this: "I do solemnly swear that I will support, obey and defend the Constitution of the United States and the Constitution of this Commonwealth. And I will discharge the duties of my office, with fidelity."

After taking that oath, the new Mayor vanished amongst the crowd ceding the spotlight to the Council members who were about to do the same. But the assembly wouldn't allow for such humbleness. The wild standing ovation that followed forced him back out front with a shy smile and uncomfortable hand wave.

When the crowd dispersed, Papenfuse had a surprise for the media. He took us deep within the city government building to show us the true extent of its deterioration. For the first time, the public got to see decades old rotting carpet, cracked floors and ceilings. The public safety building had missing tiles, exposed wires and dripping water. The building was so bad, police had to cover their paperwork and criminal evidence for fear of something falling from the ceiling. It was obvious this blight was not new, just not known.

"I'm not nervous, but I do feel the weight of all that needs to be done," Papenfuse told the press afterward. "So many things need to be addressed."

What the public and media did regularly see, such as the Mayor's suite, atrium and exterior aesthetics, looked great.

"This demonstrates our priorities, which I'm trying to change." The new mayor announced he had set up a fund for outside donors to help with repairs.

When Papenfuse entered his new office for the first time as mayor, awaiting him lay a letter from his predecessor, who had missed the inauguration. The contents of that letter remain known to only a few.

At that moment, for the first time since arriving in Harrisburg in September of 2010, I finally felt the city had a promising future. Bankruptcy may still be in its future. But by early 2014, Pennsylvania's capital at least had a fighting chance. This optimism was not only mine; you could sense city and suburban residents felt anew with confidence.

I'm sure "The Strong Plan" will not be perfect. There will be issues along the way. The drastic rise in parking fees and fines are already taking a toll on downtown businesses. But given the uncertainty of the alternative, it seemed a minor inconvenience. Also, for the time being, crime was down—especially violent crime. But there were still no indictments against those who so violently murdered the city.

Papenfuse's first few weeks in office were cluttered with press conferences announcing new hires and new initiatives. He proved equally as ambitious as his predecessors, though with an ostensibly contrary aura.

My investigative reports during the city's financial collapse, in part, convinced my bosses to promote me to full-time investigative reporter. As much as I loved my new role, I did miss the day-to-day interactions of city politics. On the rare occasion I got a chance to cover the city, I felt lost. So much had changed so quickly. The mood. The conversation. The atrium air even seemed afresh. At mayoral pressers, I barely recognized any faces or names. There were some familiar hands to shake, but not many. The city had moved on without me.

By early spring, Mayor Papenfuse was molding the city to his liking. Following one of his many media briefs, I took a few minutes to reacquaint myself with some old friends from the collapse days. The conversations were brisk, but meaningful. When the atrium emptied, I found myself largely alone. With my photographer in the truck ingesting the video, I took a second to admire the peace. Over the previous three-and-a-half years, I spent a lot of time in that atrium. Some of it exhausting. Most of it chaotic. All of it extraordinary.

It was in that atrium where I formulated many of my questions about Mayor Reed, the incinerator and Mayor Thompson. And standing in that atrium on that day, I can honestly say all of them had been answered.

Content in the moment, I noticed the bathroom near Council chambers I would frequent prior to those long, boring meetings. Since I had some time, I made my way over.

As I suspected, the room was empty. When I stepped to the sink to run some water over my hands, I immediately spotted that familiar crack in the mirror. It had now stretched across the length of the glass, perhaps to grow no more.

With my hands clean, I turned to the wall and grabbed a paper towel. Once the moist ball lay at the bottom of the trash can, I opened the door, walked through the atrium, and went about my life.

REFERENCES

Paul Beers, *City Contented, City Discontented: A History of Modern Harrisburg* (Harrisburg: Midtown Scholar Press, 2011)

Charles Dickens, *American Notes* (England: Chapman & Hall, 1842), Chapter 10

Frederick Douglass, *The Frederick Douglass Papers: 1842-1852 (New Haven: Yale University, 2009) 223*

Major William T. Gillespie, Jr. "Logistics and Lee's Antietam Campaign," Army Logistics University, JanFeb 2003

Luther Reily Kelker, *History of Dauphin County, Pennsylvania* (New York: The Lewis Publishing Company, 1907) 622

John George Nicolay, *A Short Life of Abraham Lincoln (UK: Dodo Press, 2007) 171*

"Paxton Boys," http://www.u-s-history.com/pages/h1188.html

James Roxbury, "Harrisburg Mayor Thompson on Postponing the Eastern Sports and Outdoor Show: 'It's Sending NRA a Loud Message," Roxbury News, January 24, 2013

John Weldon Scott, *African Americans of Harrisburg* (Harrisburg: African American Museum of Harrisburg Inc., 2005) 19

Sharon Smith, "On Harrisburg Mayor Linda Thompson's inauguration day, history and celebration trump politics and rivalries," PennLive, January 4, 210

Charles Thompson, "'I'm staying,' Harrisburg Mayor Linda Thompson tells crowd of 250 at unprecedented rally," PennLive, February 15, 2011

Cooper H. Wingert, *The Confederate Approach on Harrisburg: The Gettysburg Campaign's Northernmost Reaches* (UK: The History Press, 2012)

William Henry Wilson, *The City Beautiful Movement* (Baltimore: Johns Hopkins University Press, 1989) 139

ABOUT THE AUTHOR:

Photo by Ron Mounts

Chris Papst is a multiple Emmy-award winning investigative reporter whose work has initiated changes in law and sparked criminal investigations. He currently works at ABC 7/WJLA in Washington, DC.

CPSIA information can be obtained at www.ICGtesting.com
Printed in the USA
BVOW11*1647270515

402100BV00012B/128/P

9 781620 065914

JUN -- 2015